Entertaining with
Regis & Kathie Lee

Entertaining with
Regis
&
Kathie Lee

~❦~

Year-Round
Holiday Recipes,
Entertaining Tips,
and Party Ideas

Regis Philbin & Kathie Lee Gifford

with Barbara Albright

❦HYPERION

New York

Grateful acknowledgment is made for permission to reprint the following:

Clever Shrimp Diego, Flaming Bananas Brisbanne, Marinara Sauce, Marinated Shrimp Kebabs, Spring Bada-Bing Lamb Chops: © Casslee Corporation D.B.A. Clever Cleaver Productions

Penne with Shrimp and Asparagus: © Maria Di Saverio, owner Tre Scalini Restaurant

Potato pancake recipes: Original recipes by Rozanne Gold, author of *Little Meals: A Great New Way to Eat and Cook* (Villard Books)

Entertaining tips from Rozanne Gold's *Little Meals: A Great New Way to Eat and Cook* (Villard Books)

Kermit the Frog's Shoofly Pie for Humans: © 1993 Jim Henson Productions, Inc. "Muppets," "Muppet Press," and character names and likenesses are trademarks of Jim Henson Productions, Inc.

Passover Potato Pudding: From *Jewish Cooking in America* by Joan Nathan. © 1994 Joan Nathan. Reprinted by permission of Alfred A. Knopf, Inc.

Rice Calabrese Style, Italian Pastera: © 1991 Joseph E. Orsini

Vegetable Soufflé, Linguine with White Clam Sauce: © Nicola Paone

Bronzed Chicken Breasts: © 1989 Paul Prudhomme

Crawfish and Corn Maque Choux: © 1984 Paul Prudhomme

Midtown Meat Loaf: © 1991 Paul Prudhomme

Buffalo Chicken Wings: © Rootie's and Rootie's Foods International, Inc.

Suppa 'i Pisci: From *Papa Andrea's Sicilian Table: Recipes from a Sicilian Chef as Remembered by His Grandson*, by Vincent Schiavelli. © 1993 Vincent Schiavelli. Published by arrangement with Carol Publishing Group. A Birch Lane Press Book

Tennessee Trifle: From *The Dinah Shore American Kitchen*. Published by Doubleday. © 1990

KFC recipes from Todd Wilbur: © Penguin USA

Sylvia's World-Famous BBQ Ribs: From *Sylvia's Soul Food,* by Sylvia Woods and Christopher Styler. © 1992 Sylvia Woods. By permission of William Morrow & Company, Inc.

Blueberry Pie and Pâte Brisée: Courtesy of Martha Stewart and Clarkson Potter. All rights reserved. © Clarkson N. Potter, Inc., 225 Park Avenue South, New York, NY 10003

Copyright © 1994, Regis Philbin and Lambchop Productions

Library of Congress Cataloging-in-Publication Data

Philbin, Regis.
    Entertaining with Regis & Kathie Lee : year-round holiday recipes, entertaining tips, and party ideas / Regis Philbin & Kathie Lee Gifford; with Barbara Albright. — 1st ed.
       p. cm.
    Includes bibliographical references and index.
    ISBN 0-7868-6067-7
    1. Holiday cookery. 2. Entertaining. I. Gifford, Kathie Lee II. Albright, Barbara. III. Title.
TX739.P52 1994
641.5'68—dc20
                                      94-14787
                                      CIP

Book design by Richard Oriolo

FIRST EDITION

10 9 8 7 6 5 4 3 2 1

Contents

A Word from Regis & Kathie Lee

As with our first cookbook, this book was very much a collaborative effort.

Many thanks to all the people who have generously and enthusiastically shared their recipes and ideas with us to be included in *Entertaining with Regis & Kathie Lee*. We have enjoyed their appearances on the show and we are glad to have this book as a permanent record of their recipes—recipes we certainly intend to use when we entertain in our own homes. Our gratitude, too, to the publishers and restaurants who have given us permission to reprint the recipes.

Thanks are also due to Mary Kellogg, Robin Shallow, and Taryn Johnson of Buena Vista Productions for their commitment to this

Regis and Kathie Lee, America's favorite morning team.

cookbook. We could never have done it without their organized record-keeping of all the guests who have appeared on "Live."

Special credit also goes to Rhonda Brown for her valuable editorial input and to Lynn Albright, Isabelle Vita, Leslie Weiner, and Michael Yamrick for their careful testing to make sure that all the recipes work perfectly. Thank you, too, to Ted, Samantha, and brand-new baby Stoney Westray, for letting us borrow your wife and mother, Barbara Albright, to be our editor (with special thanks to Stoney for being such an even-tempered newborn).

With pleasure, we credit the whole "Live" crew—executive producer Michael Gelman and the production staff: Barbara Fight, Kathleen Gold-Singer, Suzy Hayman-DeYoung, Rosemary Kalikow, Cynthia Lockhart, Cindy MacDonald, David Mullen, Isabel Rivera, Joanne Saltzman, Robin Shallow, Delores Spruell-Jackson, and John Verhoff. Their recipes, entertaining tips, and general support are all terrific.

Thanks also to Jim Griffin, our agent, for once again putting the group together for this second volume of recipes.

And our gratitude to Leslie Wells, our editor at Hyperion, and her extremely helpful assistants, Carla Byrnes and Laurie Abkemeier, for their vision in helping us put together this book that will help us host great parties all year long.

Let the good times begin!

Introduction:
Some Host Chat from
Regis & Kathie Lee

Like every segment of "Live—With Regis & Kathie Lee," parties are productions that require careful planning, interesting guests, and top-notch ingredients. In this, our second cookbook, we have pulled together our favorite party recipes and grouped them into chapters with specific themes. Having a theme can be a building block for any party. Of course, you can mix and match the recipes to suit your own needs—whether for a particular event or as a special meal at home with your family to celebrate something as simple as the first sunny, springlike day after a harsh winter.

Most of the recipes in *Entertaining with Regis & Kathie Lee* have appeared on "Live." These recipes were demonstrated by leading chefs and cookbook authors or by celebrities who are great hosts and who cook as a hobby. However, there were also some recipes from our "family" members that were just too delicious to leave out. By "family" we are referring to members of our personal families and our extended family—the production staff of the show. Everyone involved with producing "Live" plays an important role in keeping track of the culinary happenings in America. Because of this, their personal contributions are invaluable.

In addition to recipes, we also have provided guidelines for putting together a party (beginning on page xi). At the beginning of each chapter, we offer some ideas for adding innovative flair to every party you host. Use your own ingenuity to expand on these ideas to suit your own needs and set the mood. Throughout the book, you will find information about our personal party experiences as well as our thoughts on what makes a great party. We have also included some of our favorite photos from the show.

If you approach the idea of hosting parties with trepidation because you are worried about coping with the unexpected, take heart. Keep in mind that five days a week we host a *live* television program, always knowing that *anything* could happen. So it's important to keep things in perspective and not take any minor mishaps too seriously. Making a joke about the faux pas is usually how we handle the situation.

Use this book for its wonderful recipes and to help provide inspiration and guidance for your own parties. As you prepare your guest list, remember—as we do when we schedule guests for "Live—With Regis & Kathie Lee"—to invite the people you *really* want to entertain. These people are the true focal point, both of parties and of live television programs. Last but not least, remember to have a great time at your own party. If you're having fun, there's a pretty good chance that your guests will, too.

Cheers!

Planning a Party— the Basics

Parties can be small—for instance, simple celebrations with your immediate family—or they can be large affairs. There can be a reason for a party, such as a seasonal holiday, or you can create the reason out of your own imagination, such as a bash for beating the winter blahs. Building your party around a theme helps to coordinate all aspects of your get-together. Think about your favorite parties. What was it about them that made them so special? No matter what kind of party you are having, there are a few basics that you need to consider so that you will be able to enjoy your party as much as your guests.

Planning

Planning and list-making are the two most important details to attend to when giving a party, no matter how casual it is. The time you spend plotting out your event on paper can do much to ensure against chaos and can help you come off as a relaxed host or hostess in complete control. Your mood sets the tone for everyone else.

Whether in doubt or not, make a list and plan *every* detail. In fact, make separate lists for each aspect of the party! Make lists for groceries and other items you will need; break down the steps for food preparation and itemize when each step must be done; plan in your mind which plates, platters, and serving utensils you will be using—perhaps labeling each one with a stick-on note. Plan where each item will be placed when you serve it, and think about how you will garnish each dish. If necessary, contact a friend for additional refrigerator or freezer space you can use for make-ahead dishes or storage on the day.

Design a master timetable and do as much as you can ahead of time, starting as early as possible to prevent last-minute rushing around. Plan to have something cooking when your guests arrive; a delicious aroma creates a warm welcome.

Tips for Entertaining
~❦~

Regis: We prefer to entertain a small group of people so you get to spend time with everyone. If it's a sit-down dinner at one table, it's always wise to have one or two good storytellers to keep the conversation lively. I'm only one man—I can't do it all!

Kathie Lee: Never invite anyone you don't really want. Never invite someone out of guilt. If you do, it will put a strain on the party itself. Surround yourself with people you love and food you love. It's so simple, if you refuse to let politics get in the way. Your mother will say, "You know, you really *should* have Aunt Beth." But maybe you don't want Aunt Beth. Don't let your mother make you feel obliged or guilty. Do what's right in your own heart.

The more you are in control, the better prepared you will be to handle the unexpected. The unexpected *will* happen, but when the overall plan is firmly in place and you've got a smile on your face, you will be able to pull off the event with style and finesse. When you give it your best shot, everyone will appreciate your efforts. Never apologize. Even mistakes can make for a memorable party! When everyone has gone home and everything is tidy once again, put all your recipes and notes in a file folder or a notebook for easy reference the next time you are getting ready to host a party.

The Guests
~❦~

Using Regis and Kathie Lee's advice that you invite only the people you *want* to invite, be sure to include a few people who are good raconteurs, and think about people who are congenial. Also plan for the number of people your budget and space will accommodate. Invite enough people for good cheer, but not too many for comfort.

The Invitations
~❦~

Whether you invite people by phone or send out written invitations, you should invite your guests well ahead of time. Make sure to include all the pertinent information: date and time, location (and a map if necessary), theme, if there is one, and any special instructions. Ask for a reply in those terms—some people don't seem to know anymore what R.S.V.P. *means.* If you don't get replies, give people a call and find out if they are coming.

Obviously, if you are planning a simple event for your immediate family, you can skip this step. However, it could be fun to send out little notes to family members, telling them about a party for a special celebration such as a birthday or anniversary.

The Setting
~❦~

Depending on the event, your imagination, and your energy level, you can create an atmosphere exactly as simple or as extravagant as you wish. Obviously, more imagination and energy will save you money.

Take a fresh look at the space you are planning to use for the party. Perhaps it can be rearranged to better accommodate the people and your plans. Think about where everyone will sit. Rent or borrow chairs if you need to. If it is wintertime, plan for a place where guests can put their wraps. For outdoor parties, be sure to have alternative plans for holding the party indoors if the weather is not cooperative.

In each chapter, we have given tips for interesting ways to set the table, and we have included some inspired centerpiece ideas on page xiv. Make sure that your centerpieces aren't so tall that they interfere with your guests' conversations. Many times, you can use the dessert as a centerpiece for your meal. If you are short of time, you can buy floral arrangements and rent or purchase serving platters, dishes, and linens. Beautiful glasses and dishes "say" special event.

Think about the music that you want for your event. It can be as easy as your own collection of records or CDs, perhaps chosen in keeping with the specific theme of your party. You can also hire a DJ or a band if space and your budget allow. Another idea is to hire a live performer—a guitarist, a piano player, or a string quartet. If there is a music school in your area, you may be able to hire students to perform. (Make sure to hear and see them perform first, to be confident that they are going to give you what you want. In most cases, the music should be in the background and help to provide a pleasant environment for conversation.)

The Menu
~ℓ~

We have grouped the recipes in this book under specific occasions. Of course, most of them will work well for other events, too. When planning your menu, think of your guests and any special preferences they may have. Think about what is in season and design your menu accordingly. Compose your meal so that it includes some items that are simple to prepare and others that may take a little more effort but will dazzle your guests. Think of the way the foods will look on a plate or in a buffet, and keep in mind their colors and textures, as well. These should provide pleasing contrasts and complement each other.

Remember to save some of your energy so that you can be a relaxed and participatory host. When you are short of time, don't hesitate to buy prepared items. With all your good planning and lists, try to get your shopping done as far ahead as possible, and prepare as much food in advance as you can.

Your ultimate goal is to pamper your guests so that they feel warm and welcome. You want to provide them with such a good time that they will leave with special memories of being entertained by you.

Centerpieces

Kathie Lee: I love centerpieces. I like to find an unusual object at an antique store and build flowers around it, but I'm always careful to keep the display low enough so that people can see over it. I've taken little blueberry cartons and planted fresh tulips in them.

I hate fixed bouquets. Whenever I get one, I take it apart and make smaller, more natural-looking arrangements in vases. At Christmas, I have wooden angels that I always put in the center of the table. Then Cody and I gather up holly and pine cones and arrange them all around the base of the angels.

I always try to get him involved. In the summer, when he goes on walks with Frank, he usually brings me some flowers. Sometimes they're a little wilted, but they're special to me.

Chapter 1

Hello New Year Brunch

············· ❧ ·············

What better time to have a party than on the first day of the year? If you have made New Year's resolutions to see friends more often and do more entertaining, having a brunch on New Year's Day helps to set the pace for the months ahead.

Whether people celebrated the night before or just stayed home, they will welcome an invitation to be pampered at a brunch. And for those New Year's Eve revelers who party into the next day, the recipes in this chapter could be served at a very early morning breakfast after seeing in the New Year.

Out of consideration for guests who have resolved to lose weight, eat less fat, or eat more healthfully, be sure to offer some lighter selections, such as star chef Daniel Boulud's Baked Apples with Cranberries, so you won't be blamed for sabotaging good resolutions on the first day of the year. Olympic gold medalist Matt Biondi's 5-a-Day Golden Splash is a delightful beverage packed with fresh fruit and easily made in a blender. In fact, you might want to set up a table with a blender on it, along with an attractive arrangement of the fruits that are used in the recipe. This will encourage guests to get involved as they make their own slushy drinks. Chef Tell and the Love Chef each offer their own special pancake recipes, and there is a recipe from the late Dinah Shore for a decadently delicious trifle.

If you are partied out from a frenzied holiday season, save these recipes to use for brunches you give later in the year.

What's the best party you ever threw?

~ C ~

Regis: Hmm. We used to do a lot of entertaining in California indoors and around our pool. We don't do as much in New York, because it's not as easy, I guess. We did have a good party on New Year's Day, a New Year's brunch. We had Jack Paar and Charles Grodin and a bunch of friends. It turned out to be a lovely way to start the new year. Some

"*Well, it was funny, but it wasn't that funny.*"

things we learned about those New Year's Day brunches: people aren't that punctual or hungry. Because of all the cooking Joy did over the Christmas holidays, we used a caterer, who, of course, brought too much food. The menu included a torta rustica (layers of spinach, ham, prosciutto, and cheese in a crust). I thought it was quite suspicious looking and it lived up to all my fears. First and last time we ever served that dish. Generally, guests just like to pick at their food, especially if they're recuperating from the night before.

Kathie Lee: Since Frank and I have been married, we've spent most New Year's Eves in New Orleans, because Frank hosts the Sugar Bowl for ABC Sports. While we're there we celebrate with Dan Dierdorf and Al Michaels and their beautiful wives, along with the staff and crew. We've had some pretty good bashes in New Orleans—usually at the Windsor Court. We try to make the parties black-tie events, even though the guys are working the next day. They're not wild and crazy drunken bashes, but they're fun because it's rare for all of us to get together—all three gentlemen and their wives. And I really like the wives. Linda Michaels and Debbie Dierdorf are really special ladies, and that's about the only time of the year I get to see them.

I think the most memorable party I've ever been to has to be the party in Barbra Streisand's suite after her New Year's Day performance in Las Vegas, when she had returned to performing live after twenty-eight years. It was just electric. This was my chance to finally meet the woman who has been a tremendous career inspiration to me over the years, and a personal inspiration as well. She's a motivator, and her career teaches you to believe in yourself and not let anybody else change you—you have to be true to what you are and then work your tail off.

The party was in her suite at the MGM Grand Hotel, which had just opened in Vegas. We literally had to walk over construction sites to get to the suite; that's how unfinished the hotel was. Barbra joked about it during the show.

I don't really remember what was served. I vaguely remember talking to Jay Leno before we got a chance to meet Streisand, but believe me, the food was the last thing on my mind.

What New Year's resolutions have you made?

~§~

Regis: I make my New Year's resolutions on our show. It's a fun topic and sometimes it can lead to a running gag that lasts for years. My favorite was learning to play the piano. Over the years I have inter-

---

New Year's Brunch Tips

~§~

- For a dramatic presentation of a fine vodka or liqueur: Select a bottle size that will fit comfortably in a half-gallon milk carton, leaving at least a quarter inch between the bottle and the carton. Good choices that taste best when icy cold include flavored vodkas and the Scandinavian liqueur, Aquavit. Trim the triangular top from the milk carton and place the bottle inside. Fill the carton three-quarters of the way to the top with water. Arrange a few dark branches with red berries, sprigs of holly, or rosebuds in the water between the carton and the bottle, and put the whole thing into the freezer for several hours or overnight. Check occasionally to make sure that the branches or flowers remain evenly spaced in the carton. At brunch time, simply peel off the carton and serve your well-chilled liqueur from its intriguing icy decanter. Don't forget to place a shallow dish under the ice-covered bottle, to catch the melt-down.

- If you slip a small stick of cinnamon into the brew basket of your coffee maker, it will lend a sophisticated flavor to the coffee.

- Offer a choice of orange or cranberry mimosas. Fill champagne flutes about two-thirds full with champagne. Add orange juice or cranberry juice. Garnish the edge of each glass with a strawberry and/or a slice of orange.

- Make up small loaves of quick breads for guests to take home. Wrap

---

viewed so many talented people who could play and sing and be interviewed all at the same time. I envied them and so came the resolution. I can't play like these guests yet but I must tell you, this resolution has given me so much enjoyment and a sense of accomplishment. It's been great fun and so many people have commented about my piano playing segment, I just wish I could play better.

Kathie Lee: I try not to make New Year's resolutions, because I try to

---

them in plastic wrap. Then tie a noisemaker on top of each bread with a length of curling ribbon.

- Incorporate Father Time and Baby New Year into your decorating scheme, or dress in the costumes of these characters.

- At the party you may want to feature some of the highlights of the past year: They can be your personal big events or events of worldwide importance. If you're entertaining a fairly small group and want to introduce an icebreaker, ask guests to talk about significant things that occurred in their lives in the past year.

- Include a New Year's Day walk as part of your party.

- If youngsters are going to attend your get-together, be sure to plan an activity for them. Assemble some craft supplies, such as paper, ribbons, glue, tape, and scissors, and invite each child to create a New Year's hat. Later, play some marching music and invite the kids to parade through the party sporting their newly fashioned party hats.

- You might want to start a family tradition by preparing a special New Year's Day brunch just for your family. This is an ideal time for everyone to take a look at the year just past. Why not spend some time after dinner looking through and maybe organizing the year's photographs? You could even come up with categories for the snapshots, such as "The Year's Worst Photograph," "The Year's Funniest Photograph," "The Most Memorable Photograph," etc. This is also a great day for looking at the videotapes you have created through the year.

be a disciplined person year round. I don't want to make that first-of-the-year pledge that's so impossible; I think it's a mistake. People make this enormous promise to themselves and then the rest of the year they're not able to keep it. Why should the first of the year be some magical time? I think people put an awful lot of pressure on themselves.

I did, however, make a non–New Year resolution recently to get into better shape than I've ever been in. I've had two babies now, and I've turned forty, so this was a watershed year for me. I thought, Honey, if you ain't going to do it this year, you ain't ever going to do it. So I'm working on that. I've got a trainer for the first time in my life, and I'm working hard. It helps to be doing an exercise video and know that thousands of people will see your fat thighs if you don't do it. That's the best incentive in the world.

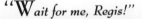

"Wait for me, Regis!"

Matt Biondi's
5-a-Day Golden Splash

At the start of a new year, many of us resolve to eat the recommended five servings a day of fruits and vegetables. Swimmer Matt Biondi, the Olympic gold medalist, prepared his special training drink for the viewers of "Live." Serve this healthy, refreshing drink whenever you are looking for a quick pick-me-up.

1 cup seedless green grapes
1 orange, peeled and cut into quarters
1 banana, peeled
1/2 cup strawberries, hulled
10 ice cubes
1 teaspoon honey

In the container of a blender, combine the grapes, orange, banana, and strawberries and process until smooth. Add the ice cubes and honey and process until mixed well.

Vegetable Soufflé

Chef Nicola Paone serves up delicious Italian food at his namesake restaurant in New York City; he also has an exquisite singing voice and regularly sings while he's in the kitchen. At your next brunch, play an Italian opera as accompaniment when you serve Nicola's vegetable-packed soufflé.

1 cup shredded lettuce
1 cup shredded chicory
1 cup shredded spinach
1 cup shredded carrots
1 cup shredded onions
4 large eggs
2 cups ricotta cheese
1 cup grated Parmesan cheese
1/4 cup chopped fresh parsley
Pinch of ground cinnamon
Salt and pepper to taste

Preheat the oven to 375°F. Butter a 2-quart soufflé or casserole dish. Lightly dust the dish with flour and tap out any excess.

Bring a large saucepot of water to a boil. Add the vegetables and cook for about 1 minute, or until they are slightly softened. Drain the vegetables well.

In a large bowl, lightly beat the eggs. Stir in the vegetables, ricotta, Parmesan, parsley, cinnamon, salt, and pepper. Pour the mixture into the prepared dish. Bake for 30 to 35 minutes, or until the soufflé is puffed and golden.

Art's Heavenly Ambrosia

Makes 6 to 8 servings

 Art Moore, director of programming for WABC, says that this easy recipe for "food of the gods" evolved from a couple of recipes he got from his mother. It's an easy combination to remember and Art likes to make it using the fruits he has on hand. We've included it in our brunch chapter, but it works equally well as a salad or dessert, and Art often serves the refreshing fruit medley at summertime barbecues. Add any or all of the optional ingredients at the end of the ingredients list.

1 cup sour cream
1 cup flaked coconut
1 cup miniature marshmallows
1 cup pineapple tidbits, drained
1 cup mandarin orange segments, drained
1 cup chopped pitted dates (optional)
1 cup seedless grapes, halved (optional)
1 cup pitted white cherries, halved (optional)
1/2 cup chopped nuts (optional)

In a large bowl, stir together all the ingredients until combined. Cover and refrigerate until ready to serve.

Apple-Nut Pancakes

If one of your New Year's resolutions is to let people know that you care, serve them these spicy pancakes created by the Love Chef, Francis Anthony, a regular guest on "Live."

1 cup all-purpose flour
1 1/2 tablespoons granulated sugar
2 teaspoons baking powder
1/2 teaspoon salt
2 apples, peeled, cored, and sliced thinly
1 cup skim milk
2 large egg whites
2 tablespoons applesauce
1 teaspoon vanilla extract
1/2 teaspoon pumpkin pie spice
1/2 cup sliced almonds or chopped pecans

In a large bowl, stir together the flour, sugar, baking powder, and salt. Stir in the apples.

In another bowl, stir together the milk, egg whites, applesauce, vanilla, and pumpkin pie spice.

Make a well in the center of the flour mixture and stir in the milk mixture, just until combined.

Spray a griddle or large skillet with nonstick cooking spray. Heat the griddle until hot. The griddle is ready when a drop of water sizzles when sprinkled on the cooking surface.

Using about 1/4 cup of batter per pancake, pour the batter onto the griddle, leaving about 1 inch between the pancakes. Cook the pancakes for 1 to 3 minutes, or until small bubbles appear. Sprinkle some of the nuts over the surface of each pancake and turn it over. Cook about 1 to 2 minutes longer, or until this side is lightly browned. Serve at once.

Emperor's Apple Pancake

Makes 4 servings

 Chef Tell Erhardt, a "Live" regular, was born in Germany and was trained in some of the finest restaurants in Europe. Chef Tell arrived in the United States at the age of 28 and has received national recognition because of his frequent television appearances. He owns a restaurant on Grand Cayman Island called Chef Tell's Grand Old House, and another in Ottsville, Pennsylvania, called Chef Tell's Harrow Inne. Chef Tell has produced video cassettes filmed in the Cayman Islands that demonstrate island-style cuisine.

1 cup all-purpose flour
3 tablespoons granulated sugar
Dash of salt
1 cup milk
2 large eggs, separated
5 tablespoons vegetable oil, divided
2 cups diced apples
1/2 cup raisins
1/2 cup slivered almonds
Confectioners' sugar for sprinkling on top of the pancake
1 to 2 tablespoons cherry brandy (optional)

In a large bowl, stir together the flour, sugar, and salt until combined. Stir in the milk, egg yolks, and 1 tablespoon of the oil. Let the mixture stand for 20 minutes.

Meanwhile, in a large grease-free bowl, beat the egg whites with an electric mixer until soft peaks start to form. Fold the whites into the flour mixture.

Heat the remaining 4 tablespoons of oil in a large skillet over medium-high heat. Add the batter to the skillet and sprinkle the apples, raisins, and almonds evenly over the surface. Cook for about 2 to 4

(continued)

Gelman's Bodacious Bagel Brunch

~℮~

When it's time for brunch, Executive Producer Michael Gelman likes to put together a plentiful buffet that includes bagels and all the fixins'. It's a great way for guests to mingle and get acquainted as they assemble their bagel masterpieces. Here are the components and Michael's special suggestions for preparation and garnishing:

The Bagel Basket. Heat an assortment of bagels and bialys without cutting them in half. Place them in a basket and cover them with a towel. They will stay soft longer if they are prepared this way than if they are individually toasted.

The Fish Plate. Arrange Nova Scotia salmon (or another type of lox that is not too salty), chubs (baby whitefish), and sable on a platter. Garnish with fresh herbs and onions. Provide a bowl of creamed herring on the side.

The Cream Cheese Assortment. The more types the merrier. Here are a few varieties to get you started; quantities are up to you.

minutes, or until lightly browned on the bottom. Carefully slide the pancake onto a plate, flip the pancake over into the pan, and cook for 2 to 4 minutes longer until it settles and is lightly browned on the bottom.

Using 2 forks, carefully pull the pancake apart into servings. Sprinkle the top of the pancake with the confectioners' sugar. Sprinkle with the cherry brandy, if desired.

Take care not to overprocess the cream cheese or it will become runny.

Herbed Cream Cheese. In a food processor, chop some fresh herbs until finely chopped. Add cream cheese and process just until combined.

Vegetable Cream Cheese. In a food processor, chop vegetables such as carrots and scallions until finely chopped. Add cream cheese and process just until combined. Season with freshly ground pepper to taste, if desired.

Caviar Cream Cheese. Stir inexpensive caviar into softened cream cheese until combined. (You can also use chopped lox.)

The Garnish Plate. Arrange sliced onions and tomatoes on a plate and garnish with fresh basil leaves.

The Eggs. Chop some onions and salami ahead of time. In a skillet, cook the onions and salami in a little butter until the onions are softened but not browned. Scramble some eggs, add them to the skillet, and cook until they are done the way you like them.

Mimosas

Extra-strong Coffee

Flaming Bananas Brisbanne

Makes enough filling for 2 servings (4 crêpes)

T he "Live" set was a jungle the day that The Clever Cleaver Brothers demonstrated this banana recipe. Steve Cassarino was dressed as a big banana and Lee Gerovitz was a big bunch of grapes. It was hard to pick them out from the tropical setting on the stage, which included palm leaves, bamboo, a hanging parrot, and a big bunch of bananas. Of course, they started out their cooking demonstration with their signature—a rap:

> We're the Clever Cleavers and we're here to say,
> Watch Regis and Kathie Lee, it's the only way,
> 'Cause it's across the country that we're gonna be
> In every home, on every TV.
> You're gonna tune us in, we're gonna turn you on,
> You're gonna love this show, you won't go wrong.
> We're a little crazy and we're really hot.
> If you had the chance, you'd wanna buy our stock.

The bananas are delicious served over vanilla ice cream and in crêpes.

1 1/2 tablespoons unsalted (sweet) butter
2 large bananas, peeled and cut lengthwise
1 tablespoon granulated sugar
1/2 cup chopped walnuts
1/4 cup raisins or currants
Dash of Angostura aromatic bitters
1/4 cup Amaretto
1 cup heavy (whipping) cream
4 Chocolate Crêpes (recipe follows)
Pinch of grated nutmeg
Pinch of ground cinnamon
Sweetened whipped cream, shaved chocolate and/or grated
  orange peel, for decoration (optional)

In a large skillet, heat the butter over medium-high heat. Add the bananas and gently toss them so that they are coated with the butter. Sprinkle the bananas evenly with the sugar. Add the walnuts, raisins, and bitters and stir the mixture gently to combine.

Remove the pan from the heat. Add the Amaretto. Flame the bananas by touching the Amaretto with a lighted match and let the flames burn down. When the flames have died down, stir in the cream.

Using a slotted spoon, carefully lift out the bananas and divide them among the prepared crêpes. Add the nutmeg and cinnamon to the liquid in the skillet and continue to cook the mixture until it starts to thicken slightly. Spoon the sauce over the bananas and fold the crêpes around the bananas. Top with whipped cream, shaved chocolate, and/or grated orange peel, if desired.

"Surf's up!"

Dinah's Tennessee Trifle

The late Dinah Shore was not only a leading female singer, national talk-show hostess, and the recipient of ten Emmy Awards but an accomplished cook, too, and appeared on "Live" to demonstrate a recipe from her cookbook, *The Dinah Shore American Kitchen*. When the Tennessee town of Winchester, near Dinah's home, celebrated its brand-new Dinah Shore Boulevard, this trifle was served to her for dessert.

The recipe is ideal for entertaining because it is best assembled the night before so that the flavors can blend.

1 package (4-serving size) vanilla instant pudding and pie
  filling
2 1/2 cups milk
2 cups apricot preserves
1/4 cup cherry-flavored liqueur
Fudge Cake (Dinah's recipe follows)
1 can (15 1/2 ounces) pitted dark cherries, drained
1 cup heavy (whipping) cream
2 teaspoons confectioners' sugar
1 teaspoon vanilla extract
1/2 cup sliced toasted almonds

Prepare the pudding according to the package directions, using the milk. Refrigerate for 30 minutes, or until slightly thickened.

Combine the preserves and liqueur and set aside. Split the Fudge Cake horizontally into 2 layers. Spread 1 layer of cake with some of the preserve mixture and place the other layer on top. Cut the cake into 2-inch squares.

Spoon a third of the pudding into the bottom of a large glass bowl with straight sides or a glass soufflé dish and top with a layer of the cake squares, pressing them down slightly. Add a layer of cherries and a layer of the preserve mixture. Then top with layers of pudding, cake, cherries, the preserve mixture, and the remaining third of the pudding. Cover and chill overnight.

Just before serving, in a cold bowl, using an electric mixer with cold beaters, beat the cream, sugar, and vanilla just until soft peaks begin to form when the beaters are lifted. Spread the whipped cream on top of the trifle. Sprinkle with the toasted almonds.

Dinah's Fudge Cake

Makes 6 to 8 servings

1 cup plus 2 tablespoons all-purpose flour
3 tablespoons unsweetened cocoa powder
1 cup granulated sugar
1/2 teaspoon baking soda
1/2 teaspoon salt
3/4 cup water
1/3 cup vegetable oil
1 large egg
1 teaspoon vanilla extract

Preheat the oven to 350°F. Lightly oil a 9-inch-square baking pan. Dust with flour and tap out the excess.

In a large bowl, stir together the flour, cocoa, sugar, baking soda, and salt. Add the water, vegetable oil, egg, and vanilla. Beat on low speed until well blended, then beat on medium speed for 2 minutes.

Pour the batter into the prepared pan. Bake for 30 to 35 minutes, or until a toothpick inserted in the center comes out clean. Transfer the cake in the pan to a wire rack and cool for 10 minutes. Invert the cake onto the rack and cool completely.

Chocolate Crêpes

Makes 10 crêpes

2 medium eggs
1 cup half-and-half
1/2 cup all-purpose flour
1 tablespoon unsweetened cocoa powder (see Note)
1 1/2 teaspoons granulated sugar
1/8 teaspoon salt
Melted butter for brushing the skillet

In a large bowl, whisk the eggs until lightly beaten. Whisk in the half-and-half. Whisk in the flour, cocoa powder, sugar, and salt until the mixture is smooth. Pass the mixture through a strainer to remove the lumps.

Heat an 8-inch nonstick skillet over medium-high heat.

Using a pastry brush or a paper towel, lightly coat the bottom of the pan with melted butter.

Add 1/4 cup of the crêpe batter to the pan and tip the pan so that the bottom is evenly coated. Pour out any excess batter. Cook for 10 to 15 seconds, or until the crêpe begins to brown, and turn it over with a heat-proof rubber spatula. Cook the second side for 5 to 10 seconds. Flip the crêpe out of the pan onto an inverted plate to cool. Repeat the process until the batter is used up. Let the crêpes cool, then stack them between sheets of waxed paper until needed. Cover and refrigerate any unused crêpes.

Note: For Orange Crêpes, replace the cocoa powder with 1/2 tablespoon of grated orange peel, added after the mixture is strained.

$\mathcal{B}$aked $\mathcal{A}$pples with $\mathcal{C}$ranberries

As these apples bake, they create an aroma that fills your house with the essence of the holidays! Chef Daniel Boulud of New York City's Restaurant Daniel made this aromatic dish that is low in calories and fat-free. After heavy holiday eating, this recipe could be just what you are looking for.

4 Golden Delicious apples
2 ounces of fresh cranberries, finely chopped
2 individual packets of sugar substitute
4 (2 1/2-by-1/2-inch) strips of orange peel
1 cup water, divided
4 cinnamon sticks

Using a sharp knife, cut a 3/4-inch wide "cap" off the top of each apple and reserve. Using a melon baller or small spoon, scoop out the core and the seeds of each apple and discard.

Divide the cranberries evenly among the cavities of the four apples. Add half a packet of the sugar substitute, a strip of orange peel, and 1 tablespoon of water to each apple. Place the caps on top of the apples.

Pour the remaining 3/4 cup of water into a baking dish that is large enough to hold the apples. Break the cinnamon sticks into pieces and sprinkle them into the water. Place the apples in the dish and either bake at 325°F. for 30 to 40 minutes or cook in a microwave oven on High for 5 to 7 minutes, or until the apples are cooked through. Place each apple on a dessert plate with the cap propped up next to the apple.

Chapter 2

Super Bowl Party Fare

.................～❦～.................

Whether you are a football fan or not, it's hard to escape the infectious spirit of the Super Bowl and the festive foods that are well suited for serving at this event.

Many of the recipes in this chapter were demonstrated on "Live" during the week before the 1993 contest between the Buffalo Bills and the Dallas Cowboys. Appropriately enough, Buffalo Chicken Wings were demonstrated by Marty Stein, the owner of Rootie's, a Buffalo-area restaurant that serves almost a ton of these fiery hot wings each week. Dean Fearing, the chef of the prestigious Mansion at Turtle Creek in Dallas, prepared his dynamite recipe for Cowboy Kick-off Coleslaw. A natural choice for Super Bowl fare is chili, and serving the following version from Chef Bobby Flay of New York City's Mesa Grill is sure to score extra points. For a memorable dessert, set up all the makings for a Super Bowl Sundae Bar. Offer guests several flavors of ice cream and a variety of help-yourself toppings such as nuts, fresh and dried fruit, granola, M&M's and other candies, sprinkles, chocolate chips, miniature cookies, sweetened whipped cream, syrups, and sauces. Mix and match the recipes in this chapter to suit your personal entertaining style.

Do you watch the Super Bowl on television, or do you prefer to be in the stadium?

~🏈~

Regis: When we lived in California, I used to go to Chasen's restaurant in Los Angeles for their Super Bowl party. Chasen's would have a lot of celebrities and athletes. I remember sitting right alongside Joe Namath, watching Joe Montana's team win the Super Bowl. Namath knew then that Montana was going to be a great quarterback.

Kathie Lee: The best place to watch the Super Bowl is at home. Actually, being there isn't all it's cracked up to be. This coming year we'll be there because ABC is covering it. It will be the 25th anniversary of Monday Night Football, so it's a very big year for Frank. I'll be there for him, and I'm sure we'll be hosting different events that ABC is involved in. Frank desperately wants me to sing the National Anthem this year, but after seeing Natalie Cole and Whitney Houston sing it the last couple of years, I don't think so.

"*I* just love this guy so much!" Regis says as he gives Michael Gelman a friendly squeeze.

Marty's Buffalo Chicken Wings

Makes 4 servings

Marty Stein, owner of Rootie's, one of the most highly acclaimed restaurants in the Buffalo area for Buffalo-style chicken wings, made these powerful chicken wings for his contribution to Super Bowl Week 1993. Appropriately enough, Buffalo, New York, is home to the Buffalo Bills, one of the competing teams.

Rootie's serves almost a ton of chicken wings a week, accompanied by "Rootie's Famous Gourmet Blue Cheese Dressing and Dip" (available in jars in the western New York area), so Marty is a seasoned pro when it comes to getting the maximum enjoyment from eating Buffalo-style chicken wings. Here is Marty's suggested chicken-wing-eating technique: "One can choose to dip them in the blue cheese dressing/dip or not to. After taking a bite of the chicken wing, one typically takes a bite of celery or carrot that has been dipped in the blue cheese dressing/dip to cool the palate. This also helps to keep the little sweat balls from forming on the upper lip, the eyes from being watery, and the nose from dripping."

For those with asbestos-lined mouths, Marty offers variations for Hot Sauce and Suicide Sauce. On "Live," Kathie Lee wanted Marty to make the sauces so suicidal that Frank, after sampling them, wouldn't leave for Japan. Marty commented, "Frank likes seriously spicy food . . . he left for Japan."

BLUE CHEESE DRESSING
1/2 cup mayonnaise
1/2 cup sour cream
4 ounces blue cheese, crumbled
1/8 teaspoon garlic powder
1/8 teaspoon onion powder

(continued)

CHICKEN WINGS

Vegetable oil for frying

2 pounds chicken wings, cut into pieces at their joints
(approximately 16 to 18 pieces after cutting them; do not
use the wing tips)

MEDIUM SAUCE

1/2 cup (1 stick) margarine

1 cup hot pepper sauce (Marty uses Frank's Hot Sauce)

1/8 teaspoon garlic powder

To Make the Blue Cheese Dressing: In a small bowl, stir together all the dressing ingredients until combined. Cover and refrigerate for at least 30 minutes to allow the flavors to blend.

To Make the Wings: Heat oil to 375°F. in a deep-fat fryer or a saucepan. Fry the wings for about 20 to 25 minutes, making sure that the wings are separated while frying.

To Make the Medium Sauce: Meanwhile, melt the margarine in a large saucepot on the stove or in a large bowl in the microwave. Stir in the pepper sauce and garlic powder. If you are using a pot, place the cooked wings in the sauce, cover the pot securely with a lid, and carefully shake the pot to coat the wings with the sauce. Or you can place the wings in the bowl of sauce and stir to coat them with the sauce. Serve with the Blue Cheese Dressing.

Variations: For Hot Sauce, add an additional 1 cup of pepper sauce to the Medium Sauce. If that is not hot enough for your palate, use the hot pepper sauce exclusively without the Medium Sauce base. For Suicide Sauce, combine 1 cup of pepper sauce, 1 cup of sliced jalapeños, and 1 teaspoon cayenne pepper and process in a blender until smooth before combining this sauce with the wings.

Making Your
Super Bowl Super

~ξ~

- Cover a buffet table with a piece of Astroturf. "Draw" yard lines with white adhesive tape.

- Decorate with the colors of the two teams that are playing. Use football-connected items to set the tone of the party.

- Make a cheese ball or a cake in the shape of a football.

- A large basket filled with breads of all sorts makes an inexpensive edible centerpiece. Mix tall French baguettes with round wheat and pumpernickel loaves, seeded bagel sticks, and any other interesting shapes and flavors you can find. Invite guests to tear off pieces during the party. To accompany the bread, set out a few saucers of good-quality oil for guests to dip the bread into. Or roast peeled garlic cloves in aluminum foil for 45 minutes and serve as a rich, low-calorie spread for the bread.

- Before the game starts, have a pool for the final outcome.

- For non-football fans, plan another activity such as learning how to knit, or needlepoint.

- Cut out and bake gingerbread "footballs." Use white icing to pipe the trim and the ties on the balls.

- If your home is fairly indestructible, have a couple of sponge-type footballs that guests can pass around during the game.

- Make up personalized football jerseys for your party, such as "Regis & Kathie Lee's Super Bowl Party."

- Consider renting a hot-dog machine, a cotton-candy machine, or a popcorn machine, just for fun.

~ξ~

Carl's Penne à la Vodka

Actor Carl Weathers appeared on "Live" to promote his television series, "In the Heat of the Night." You could tell by Carl's kitchen moves that he is quite an accomplished cook, and he said that he just has fun with cooking. Carl learned how to cook from his mother; in college, out of necessity, he became the "mamma" for his noncooking roommates. Serve this dish with an arugula salad tossed with a balsamic vinegar and olive oil dressing, and fresh garlic bread.

16 ounces penne pasta
2 tablespoons unsalted (sweet) butter
2 tablespoons olive oil
1 medium onion, chopped
4 large garlic cloves, minced
24 mushrooms, sliced
20 Italian Roma or regular tomatoes, peeled and seeded
2 bunches fresh basil, stems removed
1/4 cup vodka
1/8 teaspoon crushed red pepper flakes
Salt and pepper to taste
1/3 cup heavy (whipping) cream
Additional basil leaves, for garnish
Freshly grated Parmesan cheese

Bring a large pot of salted water to a boil. Add the pasta and cook just until al dente. Drain and keep the pasta warm.

Meanwhile, in a large skillet, heat the butter and oil over medium heat. Add the onion and garlic and cook for 5 minutes, or until the vegetables are tender.

Add the mushrooms and cook 5 minutes longer. Add the tomatoes, basil, vodka, red pepper flakes, salt, and pepper.

Simmer for 15 to 20 minutes and set aside to cool slightly. In the container of a food processor, process the mixture until it is almost smooth. Add the heavy cream and process just until combined.

Serve the sauce over the cooked pasta. Garnish with basil leaves and Parmesan cheese.

R*egis begs for mercy after trying out a few moves with The Alexis Brothers from the Cirque du Soleil.*

$\mathcal{S}$outhwestern
$\mathcal{S}$uper $\mathcal{B}$owl $\mathcal{C}$hili

Makes 8 servings

Chef Bobby Flay of New York City's Mesa Grill demonstrated this dynamite chili recipe in honor of the 1993 Super Bowl. Authentic Southwestern ingredients and Bobby's innovative culinary style make this a splendid dish for serving after a day in the brisk outdoors, whether you were watching a big game, ice skating, or skiing.

1 cup olive oil
2 1/2 pounds lamb, trimmed of visible fat and cut into
    1/2-inch cubes
1 1/2 large onions, diced
1 1/2 tablespoons finely chopped garlic
3/4 cup dark beer
1 can (16 ounces) whole tomatoes, drained and puréed
1 1/2 chipotle peppers, puréed (see Note)
1 cup ancho or regular chili powder
1 tablespoon ground cumin
2 cups chicken stock or broth
3 cups cooked or canned black beans, drained
1/2 cup honey
6 tablespoons freshly squeezed lime juice
Salt and freshly ground black pepper to taste

In a large saucepot, heat the oil over high heat. When hot, add the cubes of lamb and cook, turning frequently, until the lamb is seared on all sides.

Add the onions and garlic and cook 3 minutes longer, stirring frequently.

Add the beer and lower the heat to medium-high. Stir in the tomatoes, chipotle peppers, chili powder, and cumin. Stir and continue cooking for 10 minutes. Reduce the heat to medium, add the stock, and continue to simmer for 45 minutes. Add the beans and simmer for 15 minutes. Stir in the honey, lime juice, salt, and pepper.

Note: Jalapeños are the chilis most commonly used to make chipotles. These peppers are dried by smoking. They are available in cans at stores that carry Mexican specialty items.

Cooking Dried Beans
~&~

Dried beans must be rinsed and then soaked before they can be used in recipes. There are two methods for soaking beans—the traditional method and the quick method. Beans soaked by the traditional method retain their shapes better and have a more uniform texture.

Traditional Method: Soak the beans in cold water for 10 to 12 hours or overnight. Use at least three to four times as much water as you have beans, and change the water frequently.

Quick Method: Cover the beans with 2 inches of boiling water. Boil for 2 to 3 minutes. Cover and set aside to soak for 1 to 4 hours.

After soaking the beans, drain and rinse them, then cover with water, and cook in a pot with a lid. Bring the beans to a boil, then lower the heat, cover the pot, and simmer slowly to prevent the skins from breaking, adding more water as necessary to keep the beans covered. Most beans cook in 1 to 2 hours. Altitude, the hardness of the water, and the age of the beans will affect the length of cooking time. Do not add salt, baking soda, or acidic foods such as tomatoes or lemons until after the beans are cooked, as all of these can lengthen the cooking time.

If you are not going to use the beans right away, drain them while they are hot and store them in the refrigerator for up to 5 days. You can also freeze drained beans in small containers. To thaw the beans, place the containers in warm water or defrost them in the microwave.

Chef Paul's Midtown Meat Loaf

Makes 6 to 8 servings

 Cookbook author Chef Paul Prudhomme, of the trend-setting K-Paul's Louisiana Kitchen in New Orleans, prepared this very special recipe for the viewers of "Live." In it Chef Paul demonstrates his savvy with making a flavor-packed seasoning mix. (Make some extra mix for other uses. In fact, it's great sprinkled on top of the meat loaf.) Chef Paul's own line of seasonings, Magic Seasoning Blends, can be substituted for the seasoning mix.

SEASONING MIX

2 teaspoons dry mustard
2 teaspoons paprika
1 1/2 teaspoons salt
1 1/2 teaspoons dried thyme leaves, crushed
1 1/2 teaspoons dried basil leaves, crushed
1 teaspoon ground black pepper
1 teaspoon garlic powder
1 teaspoon onion powder
1/2 teaspoon ground white pepper

MEAT LOAF

8 slices of bacon, diced
1 1/2 cups chopped onions
1 cup chopped green (or another color) bell peppers
1 cup chopped celery
4 bay leaves
1 cup tomato juice
1/2 cup evaporated milk
2 pounds ground beef
2 large eggs, lightly beaten
1/2 cup unsalted Saltine cracker crumbs

To Make the Seasoning Mix: In a small bowl, stir together all of the seasoning mix ingredients.

To Make the Meatloaf: Preheat the oven to 350°F. Spray a 13-by-9-inch baking pan with nonstick cooking spray.

In a large skillet, over medium heat, cook the bacon until it is crispy. Using a slotted spoon, remove the bacon from the skillet, leaving the bacon drippings in the skillet.

Add the onions to the skillet and cook for 7 to 10 minutes, or until golden brown. Add the peppers, celery, bay leaves, and 2 tablespoons of the seasoning mix. Cook, stirring occasionally, for 4 minutes. Add the remaining seasoning mix and cook, stirring, for 5 minutes. Remove the skillet from the heat and discard the bay leaves.

In a large bowl, stir together the tomato juice, evaporated milk, and the bacon. Add the vegetable mixture and stir to combine.

In another large bowl, stir together the meat, eggs, and cracker crumbs until combined. Add the vegetable mixture and mix everything together.

Turn the mixture into the prepared pan and shape it into a loaf. Bake for 30 minutes. Turn the pan around and bake for 15 minutes longer, or until cooked through.

Southwestern Chicken Casserole

Makes 8 servings

Free-lance segment producer John Verhoff and his wife, Laura, love to entertain. The recipe that follows is one that John adapted from a recipe that was used in a cooking segment. He says that it's easy to expand on, and a tossed salad is the ideal accompaniment. When John and Laura entertain, they try to have everything done ahead of time so it looks effortless. They also do a trial run of recipes before serving them to guests.

1 1/2 pounds cooked boneless and skinless chicken, torn into bite-size chunks
1 package (8 to 12) corn tortillas, torn into bite-size pieces
1 medium onion, chopped
2 cups grated longhorn or cheddar cheese
1 can (10 3/4 ounces) cream of mushroom soup
1 can (10 3/4 ounces) cream of chicken soup
1 can (10 ounces) tomatoes with chilies
1/2 cup chicken stock or broth
Tabasco pepper sauce to taste
Unsalted tortilla chips for sprinkling on top (optional)

Preheat the oven to 350°F.

In a 13-by-9-inch baking dish, layer half of the chicken, half of the tortillas, half of the onion, and half of the cheese. In a medium bowl, stir together the soups, tomatoes with chilies, stock, and pepper sauce until combined. Pour half of this mixture evenly over the casserole. Repeat the layers with the remaining ingredients.

Cover and bake for 1 hour. Uncover and bake for 30 minutes longer. If desired, break up the tortilla chips and sprinkle them over the casserole about 15 minutes before it finishes baking. Let the dish stand for about 10 to 15 minutes before cutting into servings. Cover and refrigerate any leftovers for reheating the next day.

Tostones
(Fried Green Plantains)

Makes 4 servings

 sabel Rivera, "Live" 's audience coordinator, is of Puerto Rican heritage and she wanted to share her recipe for this classic Spanish snack food and side dish. Plantains are a tropical starchy banana-shaped fruit, often used in place of potatoes.

4 green plantains
Vegetable oil for frying
Salt (optional)
Finely chopped garlic (optional)

To prepare the plantains: Slice the plantains in half and peel the skins off. If desired, slice off the ends to make it easier to peel them. Reserve the skins. Cut the plantains diagonally into slices—either very thin, so they are similar to potato chips, or thicker (about 1/2 inch, which is the way Isabel prefers them).

Fill a heavy skillet with two inches of vegetable oil and heat until very hot (about 375°F.) Fry the plantains for about 5 minutes, turning occasionally, until lightly browned on both sides. Using a slotted spoon, remove the fried plantains to a plate to cool.

Place each piece of plantain in between two plantain skins. Using the palm of your hand, apply pressure until each piece is flattened. Return the plantains to the skillet and refry for 5 minutes longer, or until they are golden brown. If desired, season with salt or garlic.

The Fungiburger

There is more than one way to make a burger, as John Gottfried, one of the partners of the Gourmet Garage, so deliciously demonstrated on "Live." As many vegetarians know, mushrooms have a meaty flavor and texture, and these inspired sandwiches prove it. John, known as Mr. Mushroom, started as an amateur mycologist, and was the first large-scale distributor of wild mushrooms in the United States. The Gourmet Garage, located in the SoHo area of New York, sells mushrooms, fresh produce, and specialty foods at discount prices.

1 1/2 pounds large mushrooms, such as portobello
6 tablespoons olive oil, divided into 3 parts
1 tablespoon finely chopped shallots
1 garlic clove, finely chopped
1 tablespoon fresh thyme leaves
Juice of 1/2 lemon
Salt and pepper to taste
4 hard rolls
1 bunch of arugula

Twist off the mushroom stems and chop into 1/4-inch pieces.

In a small pan, heat 2 tablespoons of oil over medium-high heat. Cook the shallots and garlic for about 1 minute, or until translucent.

Add the mushroom stems and thyme and cook for about 2 minutes, or until the stems are browned. Squeeze the lemon juice over the stems and season with salt and pepper.

In a large pan, heat 2 tablespoons of the oil over medium-high heat. Add the mushroom caps, cover, and cook for about 5 minutes, turning once.

Preheat the broiler. Slice the rolls in half. Using your fingertips, hollow out the insides of the tops and bottoms and discard the insides. Lightly brush the hollowed-out spaces with the remaining 2 tablespoons of oil. Place the rolls under the broiler and broil until they are golden brown. Keep warm.

Spoon some of the stem mixture into each mushroom cap and place the filled caps in the hollows of the bottom halves of the rolls. Top each sandwich with some arugula leaves and cover with the roll tops.

Regis takes on a serious tone when he plays the piano.

rancis Anthony, the Love Chef, scored big points when he demonstrated this incredible recipe for potatoes on "Live." As possible toppings for his version of twice-baked potatoes, Francis suggests: sour cream—regular or low-fat, diced pepperoni, chopped artichoke hearts, crabmeat, chopped roasted red peppers, chopped jalapeño peppers, guacamole, and cooked black beans. Kathie Lee and her husband, Frank, were the co-hosts that day and they both thanked the Love Chef for his many wonderful contributions over the ten years he has been appearing on the show.

> 8 large baking potatoes, scrubbed
> Olive oil for brushing on the broiler
> 2 cups shredded low-fat sharp cheese
> 1/2 bunch of scallions, thinly sliced, including the tender
>   green tops
> 1 tablespoon prepared horseradish
> 1 teaspoon caraway seeds
> 1 teaspoon hot pepper sauce (or to taste)
> 1/8 teaspoon ground white pepper
> 1 or 2 dashes of Worcestershire sauce

Preheat the oven to 425°F. Prick each potato with the tines of a fork. Bake for about 1 hour and 15 minutes, or until the potatoes "give" when squeezed.

Cut the potatoes in half lengthwise. Carefully scoop the flesh out of each potato half and place it in a bowl. Mix in the remaining ingredients until combined.

Meanwhile, using a paper towel, lightly rub a little olive oil on the broiler pan. Position this 5 to 6 inches away from the heat source. Preheat the broiler. Arrange the skins on the prepared pan and place them under the broiler for several minutes, or until they are crisp. Remove the skins and fill each half with some of the filling mixture. Return the skins to the 425°F. oven and bake for another 5 to 10 minutes, or until they are heated through.

Executive Producer Michael Gelman and Regis confer before going on the air.

Grilled Chicken Breast with Sweet Corn–Apple Relish and Barbecued Fire-Roasted Onions

Makes 4 servings

SWEET CORN–APPLE RELISH

Freshly squeezed lemon juice
1 cup diced red apple
1 cup diced Granny Smith apple
3 ears fresh sweet corn
2 tablespoons bacon fat
1 small white onion, peeled and diced
1/4 cup diced red bell pepper
1/4 cup diced green bell pepper
1 tablespoon sweetened rice wine vinegar
1 1/2 teaspoons white wine vinegar
Salt to taste

BARBECUED FIRE-ROASTED ONIONS

12 medium onions, peeled
1 cup ketchup
1/4 cup Worcestershire sauce
Juice of 1/2 lemon (or to taste)
2 tablespoons molasses
2 tablespoons chicken or beef stock or broth
1 tablespoon malt vinegar
2 teaspoons Creole mustard
1 teaspoon Tabasco pepper sauce
1 garlic clove, finely chopped
Salt and freshly ground black pepper to taste

GRILLED CHICKEN BREASTS

4 whole boneless, skinless chicken breasts
2 tablespoons peanut oil
Salt and freshly ground black pepper to taste

To Make the Sweet Corn–Apple Relish: Add a little lemon juice to a bowl of water and place the diced apples in the water to prevent the apples from turning brown.

Using a sharp knife, remove the kernels from the corn cobs. Reserve the kernels. With the back of the knife, scrape the pulp from the cobs and reserve it separately.

In a medium skillet, heat the bacon fat over medium heat. Add the corn kernels and cook, stirring constantly, for about 5 minutes, or until the kernels turn a bright yellow. Do not brown. Add the onion, bell peppers, and reserved corn pulp and cook for 5 minutes. Add the vinegars and simmer for 4 minutes, or until the liquid is reduced. Remove the skillet from the heat. Season with salt and lemon juice. Drain the apples well and add them to the relish. Stir gently to combine. Serve at room temperature.

To Make the Barbecued Fire-Roasted Onions: Using a paper towel, lightly rub a little vegetable oil on the grill or broiler pan. Position this 5 to 6 inches from the heat source. Preheat the grill (or broiler). Arrange the onions on the prepared grill and grill or broil them slowly, turning occasionally, for about 15 minutes, or until they are lightly charred on all sides.

Preheat the oven to 375°F. Place the onions in a small roasting pan. Combine the remaining ingredients and pour the mixture over the onions. Cover and bake for about 30 minutes, turning the onions once, halfway through the cooking time. Remove the pan from the oven and keep warm.

Meanwhile, to Make the Grilled Chicken Breasts: Brush the chicken breasts with the oil and season with salt and pepper. Grill or broil the chicken breasts on the prepared grill for about 5 to 7 minutes. Turn and cook for about 5 minutes longer, or until the juices run clear. Serve the chicken breasts with the relish and onions.

Cowboy Kick-off Coleslaw

Chef Dean Fearing of the highly esteemed Mansion at Turtle Creek in Dallas, Texas, demonstrated his own style of cowboy cooking in the week preceding the 1993 Super Bowl game between the Buffalo Bills and the Dallas Cowboys. On "Live," four days before the big game, Dean accurately predicted that the Cowboys were going to win. Dean wore Cowboy quarterback Troy Aikman's "18" football jersey, and Dick Smothers was the host. Following the recipe for Southwestern-style coleslaw that Dean demonstrated on the show is an inspired recipe for chicken that he suggested as an accompaniment to it. Serve both of these recipes at a Super Bowl get-together, but also keep them in mind for your next outdoor barbecue.

> 5 cups cabbage, cut into julienne strips
> 1/2 red bell pepper, cut into julienne strips
> 1/2 yellow bell pepper, cut into julienne strips
> 1/2 carrot, cut into julienne strips
> 1 cup mayonnaise
> 2 jalapeños, chopped
> 1 garlic clove, finely chopped
> 1 tablespoon chopped fresh coriander leaves
> 1 tablespoon maple syrup
> 1 1/2 teaspoons vinegar
> 1 1/2 teaspoons Dijon-style mustard
> 1 1/2 teaspoons Worcestershire sauce
> 1 teaspoon chili powder
> 1 teaspoon ground cumin
> 1/2 teaspoon ground coriander
> Freshly squeezed lime juice to taste

In a large bowl, toss together the cabbage, peppers, and carrot until combined.

In the container of a food processor or blender, process the remaining ingredients until smooth. Pour the dressing over the vegetables and toss to combine.

Y ou probably have the ingredients on hand to make some of these irresistible chips right now! This recipe from Jonathan Fox, executive chef-partner of Papagus Greek Taverna in Chicago, Illinois, can be adjusted to make any amount and you can use as many of the toppings as you feel like. On the show, Kathie Lee was slicing the bread too thick so Jonathan joked that she was making toast instead of thin chips. No matter how you slice it, this simple snack item would make a super addition to your next Super Bowl get-together. As this recipe demonstrates, Jonathan advises that you keep your menu simple and clean up as you go, so that you can enjoy the party as well.

Italian bread
Unsliced rye bread
Olive oil, butter, or margarine

POSSIBLE TOPPINGS
Garlic powder
Dried oregano leaves
Dried thyme leaves
Grated Parmesan cheese
Sesame seeds
Cayenne pepper
Celery seeds
Crumbled blue cheese
Pine nuts
Finely chopped fresh basil leaves
Finely chopped fresh coriander leaves
Finely chopped garlic cloves
Bacon bits

(continued)

Preheat the oven to 400°F. Cut the bread into *thin* slices.

Lightly brush the bread slices on both sides with olive oil, butter, or margarine and place them on a baking sheet. Sprinkle the slices on both sides with all or some of the topping ingredients and bake for about 6 minutes, turning once, or until lightly browned and crisp.

Banana Chocolate Chip Cake

Makes 12 servings

Kathleen Gold-Singer is "Live" 's manager of on-air promotion, and this moist banana cake is one of her favorite cakes. It's based on her sister's recipe, but because Kathleen is a chocolate lover, she added the chocolate chips. Kathleen makes this when she has very ripe bananas on hand.

2 cups all-purpose flour
1 teaspoon baking powder
1/2 teaspoon baking soda
1/2 teaspoon salt
1/3 cup unsalted butter (sweet), softened
1 cup granulated sugar
2 1/2 to 3 ripe large mashed bananas
2 large eggs, lightly beaten
1 teaspoon vanilla extract
1/2 cup sour cream or plain low-fat yogurt
2/3 cup miniature semisweet chocolate chips

Preheat the oven to 350°F. Butter a 13-by-9-inch baking pan.

In a large bowl, sift together the flour, baking powder, baking soda, and salt.

In another bowl, using a handheld electric mixer, cream together the butter and sugar until combined. Beat in the bananas until combined. Beat in the eggs and vanilla, beating well.

Beat the flour mixture into the butter mixture until combined. Stir in the sour cream or yogurt. Stir in the chocolate chips.

Scrape the batter into the prepared pan. Bake for 45 to 50 minutes, or until a toothpick inserted in the center comes out clean. Transfer the cake to a wire rack and cool completely.

Chapter 3

Let's Celebrate Romance—Happy Valentine's Day

·············· ～❦～ ··············

V alentine's Day is for lovers—a day when we celebrate romance or create romance. Even the most tailored person tends to loosen up and become a little more "Victorian" in outlook for this occasion, and may even be seen sporting lace and frills.

Whether you are entertaining just one special person, creating a festive meal for your family, or even hosting a gathering of "lonely-waiting-to-be-claimed-hearts," create an atmosphere that evokes romance. Some tips follow; the rest is up to your guests.

What parties do you specially remember?

~♥~

Regis: Every year we go to the Alzheimer's Ball. One thing I like about the event is that they always have a theme. One year it was "The Lady In Red." Every woman there wore a red gown. It was interesting: There were very few duplicates. I think red is a very becoming color on a woman, and everybody looked fabulous.

Creating the Potential for Romance

~♥~

- Hearts are, of course, the natural motif for the day. If you are entertaining a bunch of singles, broken hearts could be another, different look! (You could hand out Band-Aids.) Ask everybody to tell about the worst date they ever had.

- Serve appetizers that have a reputation as aphrodisiacs. Include little tented cards that describe their purported powers.

- Make a romantic Valentine bouquet.

- Start a collection of dishes that are trimmed with hearts and lace or are heart-shaped.

- Red, white, pink, and gold lace doilies create a romantic, Victorian feeling.

- Serve a heart-shaped dessert, such as a cake baked in a heart-shaped pan, or heart-shaped cookies. For instance, heart-shaped sugar cookies dusted with powdered sugar look lovely next to a stemmed glass filled with raspberries and strawberries.

Kathie Lee: One of the greatest parties in my life was the book party that my dear friend Claudia Cohen gave me when my autobiography came out. I had been to many fabulous events in honor of other people, but I don't remember ever having one thrown in honor of me until she gave this party. It was so star-studded that I was the least of the celebrities in the room.

She took L'Orangerie, the private room at Le Cirque, and the florist, Robert Isabelle, made the room look like Central Park in the fall. It was one of the most beautiful rooms I've ever seen in my life.

- Serve champagne garnished with a strawberry.

- For a child's party, play "pin-the-heart-on-a-clown."

- Ask your guests to dress in red, or to come in Valentine-theme costumes.

- Have a party where everyone brings their most eligible friend of the opposite sex.

- Serve blush wine.

- Make or order a heart-shaped pizza.

- Dip strawberries (preferably long-stemmed) in chocolate.

- If you have a friend who's a computer "hacker," devise a compatibility questionnaire for guests to fill out before the party. When they arrive, introduce them to the "date" the computer picked.

- Toss a rosy salad with radicchio, red butter lettuce, and red oak leaf lettuce. Use red wine vinegar to make the vinaigrette dressing.

- Make a batch of long-stemmed cookies by baking your favorite recipe, cut into heart or flower shapes, and adding long stems, bought from a craft or artificial flower supply store.

At my table I had Alan Alda on my left and Mayor Dinkins on my right. Everybody said it was one of the only times they'd seen the mayor stay for an entire evening. It was just wonderful. Neil Sedaka sang. Mac Davis was doing Will Rogers on Broadway, and he performed. Marla Maples and Donald Trump came—Donald was with a date, but we know it all had a happy ending, so that's OK. Shirley MacLaine was there—I couldn't believe it. I sang—they begged me; who could stop me?—and it was just a wonderful, magical night.

I loved Claudia for caring about me that much. For her birthday the next year, Frank and I gave her a dinner party at our apartment in New York, just to let her know how special it feels.

How do you celebrate Valentine's Day, anniversaries, and birthdays?

~❦~

Regis: We usually go to a memorable place like The Rainbow Room or Rainbow & Stars. I took Joy there for her birthday to see Rosemary Clooney. That was fun. We try to pick a special place for birthdays and anniversaries. La Grenouille and Café des Artistes are great for Valentine's Day.

What's the most romantic Valentine's Day you've ever had, and what's the worst, and why?

~❦~

Kathie Lee: The worst Valentine's Days are always when you are alone. But ever since Frank has come into my life, they've always been special. This past Valentine's Day was hysterical. We'd had such an active year. We were both so exhausted and we'd spent so much money on our new house out in Colorado that we both decided that we're not going to give presents to one another this year. This is silly. Let's just be together as a family.

Somebody had sent us wonderful caviar and just that day we had received a beautiful bottle of Cristal champagne for Valentine's Day.

We'd gone out for a Valentine's Day lunch with our baby. We hadn't seen Cassidy in a dress for months—it was so cold this winter that we kept her in a sleeper, no matter what. But we put her in a little Valentine's dress, picked up Cody from school, and all went to Terra, one of our favorite little restaurants in Connecticut. We took our housekeepers, Ted and Frances Kessler, who are like grandparents to Cody and Cassidy, and our nanny, Christine, for a Valentine's lunch.

That night at dinner, we weren't particularly hungry but we wanted to celebrate. So I went and put on a pretty outfit that Frank had bought me at Laura Ashley. He'd broken the rule about no presents and gone to Laura Ashley to get us mommy and baby matching outfits. I put on the dress and little hat that Frank had bought me and we put a red candle in the center of our kitchen table. Of course, we fed the baby her gruel, whatever she was eating at that time, and Cody ate whatever *he* was eating.

We decided that *we* would have the caviar and champagne. We chopped the egg, we made the toast points, we cut up the onions, and we got out all the different accouterments that go with caviar. We put everything on the table. We uncorked the champagne and had the beautiful silverware and china out. Then we went to open the caviar—and it had spoiled. . . .

So what were we going to do? We decided to open up a couple of cans of sardines. So we had sardines and champagne for Valentine's Day and it didn't matter, because we love each other and we had our kids there. We laughed about it— Look how sophisticated we are— sardines and champagne, not exactly what Robin Leach had in mind. We learned an important lesson, too. Whenever you get caviar in the mail, eat it—eat it real quick, because it doesn't stay good for long.

Lobster with Thai Herbs

 Dishes featuring sauces that capture the essence of inspired blendings of fresh herbs, fruits, and vegetables are representative of the brilliant style of Chef Jean-Georges Vongerichten's cooking. His New York City restaurant, Vong, features French-accented Thai food, and the following recipe is a delicious and very special example. Look for the unusual items in Asian markets.

> 4 lobsters (1 1/2 pounds each)
> 1 teaspoon butter
> 1 teaspoon red curry paste
> 1 carrot, shredded
> 2 lime leaves or 2 tablespoons fresh lime juice
> 1 lemon grass stalk, chopped
> 2 cups of white port (or substitute sweet white wine)
> 1 Golden Delicious apple, peeled and shredded
> 2 teaspoons ground turmeric
> 1 cup heavy (whipping) cream
> 4 pieces of bok choy or Napa cabbage
> 1 tablespoon chopped fresh coriander leaves

Submerge the lobsters in boiling water for about 3 minutes. Cut the lobsters in half lengthwise.

In a large skillet, heat the butter and red curry paste over medium heat for 1 to 2 minutes. Add the carrot, lime leaves or lime juice, and lemon grass. Add the port and cook until the mixture is reduced by half. Add the apple and turmeric and continue cooking until the mixture is almost dry. Stir in the heavy cream.

Preheat the broiler and position the broiler pan about 5 to 6 inches away from the heat source. Broil the lobsters for 1 to 2 minutes, or until cooked through. Transfer the lobsters to a warm serving platter. Pour the sauce over the lobsters.

In the skillet, cook the bok choy for 1 to 2 minutes, or until it is tender. Serve the bok choy with the lobster and sprinkle it with the chopped coriander leaves.

"Let me see you smile!"

Joy's Seafood Risotto

J oy Philbin is well known as a gracious hostess and excellent cook. When people stop by, she always offers them something to eat or drink. Risotto, which is made with arborio rice, is a popular dish in Italy. Joy created this recipe after she and daughter Joanna took a trip to Italy and enjoyed many meals featuring risotto. Make sure to finish the meal with small cups of espresso coffee to add authentic Italian flair to the meal.

Here's some advice from Joy: An important part of making risotto is to stir it constantly as you add the liquids. This is not a dish you can walk away from before it reaches just the right consistency. The rice should be cooked through, but not mushy.

1/2 pound medium shrimp
1/2 cup olive oil, divided
2 garlic cloves, crushed
1/2 pound sea scallops, cut in half
1 cup minced onion
2 garlic cloves, minced
1 1/2 cups arborio rice
1/2 cup dry white wine
1 cup heated clam broth
About 2 cups of boiling water
2 tablespoons brandy or cognac
1 teaspoon salt (or to taste)
Freshly ground pepper to taste
2 tablespoons minced fresh parsley

P eel and devein the shrimp. To devein the shrimp, use the point of a sharp knife to make a shallow cut down the center back (the curved side) of each shrimp; then remove the dark vein. Rinse away any bits of the vein that remain. Cut the shrimp into 1/2-inch pieces.

I n a large heavy skillet, heat 3 tablespoons of the olive oil over medium heat. Add the crushed garlic and sauté for 2 to 4 minutes, or until lightly browned. Remove and discard the garlic. Add the shrimp and scallops and sauté for 2 minutes. Remove the shrimp and scallops from the skillet and set aside.

Add 3 more tablespoons of the olive oil to the skillet and sauté the onion and garlic for 5 to 7 minutes, or until lightly golden. Add the rice and stir constantly for 2 minutes, or until it is lightly toasted.

Stir in the wine. Cook and stir until the wine has evaporated. Add the heated clam broth and cook and stir until it is absorbed. Add 1 cup of the boiling water and continue cooking and stirring until the water is absorbed. Add additional boiling water as needed. Cook and stir for about 10 minutes. Don't let the rice get too moist. Add the reserved shrimp and scallops and the brandy or cognac. Stir in the remaining 2 tablespoons of olive oil. Season with salt and pepper. Stir in the parsley.

Kathie Lee's Early Training as a Hostess

~ ɝ ~

Kathie Lee's mother started training her girls to be hostesses at an early age. Joan recommends that you let your teenagers have a dinner party for four to six couples. She let her girls use her good china, crystal, and silverware and turned the party over to Kathie Lee and her sister, Michie. Of course, if asked, Joan would help out. Kathie Lee and Michie served their favorite recipes. For coffee, tea, and dessert, the girls often moved their guests into the living room by the fireplace. Kathie Lee says that this was her very favorite way to have her friends over.

Joanie's Sweet-n-Sour Chicken

Makes 4 servings

Here's a favorite supper party recipe of Joan Epstein, Kathie Lee's mother. This recipe was circulating on college campuses in the 1970s and was given to Joan by her daughter-in-law, Sandy. One of Joan's favorite variations is to substitute 8 ounces of barbecue sauce and fresh sliced onions for the Russian dressing and onion soup mix. She likes to serve this dish with crescent rolls, Carol's California Salad (see page 166), and a side dish of long-grain rice.

2 pounds assorted chicken pieces, with the skins removed
1 bottle (8 ounces) Russian dressing
1 jar (8 ounces) apricot preserves
1 envelope (1.15 ounces) onion soup mix
Chunks or rings of canned pineapple and sliced green
    peppers, for garnish

Preheat the oven to 350°F. Arrange the chicken pieces in a large baking dish.

In a large bowl, stir together the dressing, preserves, and soup mix. Pour 1/4 cup of water into the bottle and jar to rinse out any remaining bits of dressing and apricot preserves and add this liquid to the bowl. Pour the mixture evenly over the chicken.

Cover the chicken and bake for 1 hour. Uncover and bake for 30 minutes longer. The pineapple and green pepper can be added during the last 30 minutes.

Pasta with Marinara Sauce

Makes 4 servings

For their sixth appearance on "Live," The Clever Cleaver Brothers geared their menu to all the lovebirds getting ready to charm their "better halves" for Valentine's Day. They chose the following recipe because it passed "The Clever Cleaver S.E.E. Test"—*simple* for the chef, *easy* to prepare, and *elegant* to serve.

This segment started a new catchphrase for The Clever Cleaver Brothers. Right before they went on the air, Executive Producer Michael Gelman asked them to come up with something that would get Regis more involved with the action. Their solution—when The Clever Cleavers said "bada-bing," Regis added "bada-boom." From that point on, whenever The Clever Cleaver Brothers said "bada-bing," the audience yelled out "bada-boom."

Their signature rap for this segment went like this:

We're The Clever Cleavers and we're here to say
Don't forget, it's almost Valentine's Day.
This meal we're gonna make for your special honey,
It's easy to prepare, it donna cost much money.
Pasta Marinara by candlelight is fine,
Trust The Clever Cleavers, it works for us all the time.

2 tablespoons olive oil
3 garlic cloves, finely chopped
12 plum tomatoes, cored and cut into 3/4-inch pieces
3 tablespoons chopped fresh basil leaves
1 1/2 teaspoons chopped fresh oregano leaves
1/4 teaspoon Angostura low-sodium Worcestershire sauce
Ground black pepper to taste
1/2 cup water
1 tablespoon tomato paste
8 ounces pasta, cooked according to package directions and
   drained

(continued)

In a large saucepot, heat the oil over medium heat. Cook the garlic for 1 to 2 minutes, or just until it starts to brown.

Stir in the tomatoes, basil, oregano, Worcestershire sauce, and pepper. Mix in the water and tomato paste. Cover and simmer for 15 to 20 minutes. Serve over the cooked pasta.

Phyllis Diller's Himalayan Aphrodisiac

Makes 4 to 6 servings

Leading funny lady and one of the first stand-up female comedians, Phyllis Diller is no stranger to the kitchen. On her worldwide travels, she has seized the opportunity to sample the cuisines of the world, and these have had a direct influence on her cooking. Phyllis made an appearance on "Live" to demonstrate one of her recipes that was selected for inclusion in a celebrity cookbook benefiting Child Help USA. This dish is based on a recipe from an Indian cookbook, which was prepared for her by one of her (many) beaux. Poppy seeds are an intriguing component of this full-flavored recipe, and they give the dish its supposedly aphrodisiacal properties. (Phyllis reports that she also uses this mixture to marinate duck, chicken, and shrimp.)

1/2 cup vinegar

16 garlic cloves, peeled

3 tablespoons poppy seeds

1 1/2 tablespoons granulated sugar

1 tablespoon lemon pulp

1 1/4 teaspoons ground ginger

1 teaspoon salt

1 teaspoon dry mustard

3/4 teaspoon ground turmeric

1/2 teaspoon ground cumin

1/2 teaspoon crushed red pepper flakes

2 pounds lean beef, pork, or lamb, cut into 1 1/2-inch cubes

1/4 cup hydrogenated vegetable shortening

4 bay leaves

2 whole cloves

1 small onion, finely sliced

1/2 cup tomato purée

In the container of a blender or food processor, combine the vinegar, garlic cloves, poppy seeds, sugar, lemon pulp, ginger, salt, mustard, turmeric, cumin, and red pepper flakes. Process at high speed for 2 or 3 minutes, until puréed.

Place the meat cubes in a large bowl and pour the blended spices over them. Cover and refrigerate for 2 hours.

In a large Dutch oven or saucepot, melt the shortening over medium heat. Add the bay leaves and cloves and cook for 3 to 4 minutes, stirring occasionally. Add the onion and cook for 5 to 7 minutes, or until the onion is softened. Remove the pot from the heat and let the mixture become lukewarm.

Return the pot to the heat and add the meat. Let simmer for about 10 to 15 minutes, stirring occasionally. Stir in the tomato purée. Increase the heat to medium and cook for approximately 1 hour, or until the meat is tender. Using a metal spoon, skim off any fat from the surface. Remove and discard the bay leaves. Serve with Rice Rajah (recipe follows).

Adding Indian Flair to Your Party

~❧~

*H*ere are some ideas on how to create an appropriate atmosphere the next time you serve Indian food:

- Elephants are a symbol of good luck in India. For a striking center-piece, place glass, ceramic, and wooden elephants from the thrift store or your own collection amidst votive candles in jewel-toned glass holders on a piece of mirrored glass. (If you're short on elephants, use more candles.) Use napkins in various jewel tones (and brass chargers, if you have them) to complete the look.

- Display brilliantly colored tropical flowers such as lobster claws and birds of paradise in tall vases for an exotic touch. Or float brightly colored flower petals in glass bowls.

- Serve raita as a refreshing accompaniment to the meal. Mix 1 cup of plain yogurt with half a cucumber that has been seeded and chopped, and add ground cumin to taste.

Rice Rajah

Makes 4 to 6 servings

This Indian-style rice is flavored with rosewater. Its mild flavor is the perfect counterpoint to the spicy flavors of the preceding stew.

1 teaspoon vegetable oil
1/2 cup sesame seeds
1 tablespoon rosewater (available at drugstores)
1 teaspoon white pepper (or to taste)
3 cups freshly cooked rice

In a small skillet, heat the oil over medium heat. Stir in the sesame seeds and cook for 1 to 3 minutes, or until the sesame seeds are lightly toasted. Stir in the rosewater and the pepper. Stir this mixture into the cooked rice and serve.

Jean-Georges Vongerichten and Regis discuss the importance of having everything ready before you begin cooking.

Gelman's Mon Cherry Duck

 hen Executive Producer Michael Gelman wants someone to be his Valentine, he knows that the best way to get a "yes" answer is to dazzle them with his culinary prowess. Michael is a big fan of crispy duck, and the following is a variation on a recipe his mother makes (and still prepares for him when he visits her). For his favorite all-American sweetheart, Michael's all-American menu includes this seductive duck recipe with a side dish that is a medley of wild rice, nuts, and cranberries; colorful julienned vegetables and a red California zinfandel complete a romantic meal. Serve Michael's menu at your next Valentine's Day rendezvous for rave reviews.

1 medium (4 1/2 pounds) duck
Salt and pepper to taste
1/2 cup orange marmalade
3 ounces orange juice concentrate
2 cans (16 ounces each) sweet cherries in heavy syrup
1/2 cup red wine or madeira
3 tablespoons firmly packed brown sugar
2 tablespoons cornstarch

Preheat the oven to 350°F. Place the duck on a rack in a roasting pan and sprinkle with salt and pepper. Roast for 20 minutes per pound. In a small bowl, stir together the marmalade and orange juice concentrate. During the last 30 minutes of roasting, raise the oven temperature to 425°F. and baste the duck with the orange mixture every 10 minutes.

Meanwhile, in the container of a blender or a food processor fitted with the metal chopping blade, process the contents of one can of cherries until the mixture is smooth.

In a medium saucepan, combine the puréed cherries, the remaining can of cherries, the wine, brown sugar, and cornstarch. Cook over medium-high heat, stirring constantly, until the mixture boils. Boil for 1 minute, or until the sauce thickens, stirring constantly.

Cut the duck into quarters and serve with the warm sauce on the side.

Honey-Roast Chicken

Makes 6 servings

Lauren Groveman's Kitchen, Inc., is a cooking school in Larchmont, New York. The school's namesake teacher appeared on "Live" and demonstrated one of her best and most versatile chicken dishes.

While many people say they hate curry, Lauren said that the subtle use of this spice blend, along with the other wonderful ingredients in the recipe, has won over many converts. Without exception, she hasn't found anyone who tasted this dish and didn't love it. Another bonus is that the recipe is very easy to make; you can prepare the dipping mixture ahead of time. About an hour before you are ready to serve dinner, you can quickly dip the chicken in the glaze, pop the baking pan in the oven, and be free to enjoy your company.

Lauren pointed out that the key to success is using a shallow baking pan with 1-inch sides. As there is a substantial amount of sauce, the pieces will bake instead of roast if you use a deeper pan. It's the amount of sauce combined with the use of a shallow pan that makes the ultimate texture of the finished chicken unique. As the pieces of chicken cook, they "self-baste" from the bottom up in a honey-rich sauce, while the low-sided pan enables the exterior of the chicken to gain better exposure to the heat, resulting in chicken that is gloriously browned on top.

Following the directions for the chicken is a recipe for the colorful rice dish that Lauren featured with the chicken on the show. Of course, she is including both recipes in her new cookbook, *Lauren Groveman's Kitchen—Nurturing Meals for Family and Friends.*

2 (3 1/2 to 4 pounds each) roasting chickens
1/2 cup (1 stick) unsalted (sweet) butter or margarine
1/2 cup finely chopped yellow onion
2 large garlic cloves, finely chopped

1/2 cup Dijon-style mustard
1/2 cup mild honey
About 1/4 cup dried currants
2 tablespoons finely chopped peach or mango chutney
1 rounded teaspoon mild curry powder
1 teaspoon salt

Remove the chicken backs and reserve (freeze) to make stock. Cut each chicken into 8 serving pieces. Rinse the chicken pieces and pat dry with paper towel.

In a 1 1/2-to-2-quart saucepan, melt the butter over medium-high heat. Cook the onion and garlic for 3 to 5 minutes, or until softened. Add the remaining ingredients except the chicken and stir until combined.

Dip each piece of chicken in the honey mixture, coating the chicken completely. Place the chicken pieces, skin side up, in a shallow baking pan. Spoon the remaining sauce over the chicken.

Place the baking pan in a cold oven and set the temperature at 400°F. Bake for about 1 hour, or until the chicken is cooked through. (If your baking pan will not accommodate all the pieces, divide them between 2 baking pans, position the oven racks in the upper and lower third of the oven, and switch the pans halfway through baking.) Transfer the chicken to a warmed serving platter. You may serve it hot, at room temperature, or slightly chilled.

Tips for Leftovers: In addition to reheating well, this chicken makes a fabulous chicken salad. Just remove the skin and tear the meat into bite-size pieces. Add some coarsely chopped Golden Delicious apples (no need to remove the peel), coarsely chopped toasted almonds, dried currants, and minced scallions. Make a dressing with mayonnaise, some Dijon-style mustard, and a touch of honey. Toss the chicken with just enough dressing to bind, and season with salt and freshly ground pepper to taste. Serve with a green salad and some crusty rolls and you've got yourself a tasty lunch or a light supper.

Long-Grain White Rice with Corn, Peppers, and Onions

Lauren likes to use nutty basmati or Texmati rice in this recipe.

2 large ears fresh corn, shucked and all silk removed or 1 can (12 to 16 ounces) corn kernels, drained or 1 box (10 ounces) thawed frozen corn kernels
3 tablespoons butter, margarine, or olive oil
1 medium yellow onion, finely chopped
2 garlic cloves, finely chopped
1 green or red bell pepper, seeded and finely chopped (or use a combination of both peppers)
4 cups rich, well-seasoned chicken stock or broth
2 cups long-grain white rice
Salt and freshly ground black pepper to taste
Additional 1 tablespoon of butter or margarine (optional)

If you are using fresh corn, after removing the husks and silk, cut the kernels from the cobs using a sharp knife (being careful not to cut into the cob itself). Place the kernels in a bowl and use the knife to scrape up and down the corn cobs, over the bowl of corn, extracting the natural corn cream. If using canned or thawed frozen corn, begin with the step that follows.

In a 2 1/2-quart heavy-bottomed saucepan, heat the butter or oil over medium-low heat. Add the onion and garlic and cook for 3 minutes. Add the green pepper and cook for about 5 minutes, or until all the vegetables are softened and very fragrant. In another saucepan, heat the chicken stock until hot.

If you are using an aromatic rice, place it in a medium-mesh sieve and rinse and drain well; if you are using long-grain converted white rice, rinsing is neither necessary nor recommended. Add the rice to the saucepan and cook over medium heat, stirring to coat the rice with the butter and vegetables. Cook for about 3 minutes, or until the rice is dry and beginning to turn golden.

Add the hot stock and return the mixture to a boil. Stir in the corn and bring the mixture back to a boil. Cover the saucepan and reduce the heat to low. Simmer over a low flame for exactly 17 minutes without lifting the lid. (If you are using an electric stove, you don't have as much control over the heat as you do with a gas stove. Lauren suggests that you heat another burner to low while your rice mixture is coming to a boil. Then, as soon as it boils and you cover the pan, you can quickly adjust the temperature by switching the saucepan to another burner.)

To serve, uncover the rice and add a generous amount of freshly ground pepper and some salt. Stir in 1 tablespoon of additional butter or margarine, if desired. Fluff the rice with a fork and cover the pan again. Allow the rice to settle for 3 to 5 minutes to absorb any excess moisture. Serve hot.

Chocolate Persuasion

Makes 4 servings

 The Love Chef appeared on "Live" during American Chocolate Week with a decadent recipe that is sure to persuade the object of your affections to be your valentine. Cups made out of chocolate are filled with a rich ricotta cheese mixture. Each cup then sits in a velvety pool of raspberry sauce. Irresistible . . .

CHOCOLATE CUPS
6 ounces semisweet chocolate

FILLING
15 ounces ricotta cheese
1/2 cup confectioners' sugar
1 ounce semisweet chocolate, grated
1 1/2 tablespoons unsweetened cocoa powder
1 teaspoon vanilla extract

CHOCOLATE-RASPBERRY VELVET SAUCE
1/4 cup raspberry jam
1 tablespoon granulated sugar
1 tablespoon unsweetened cocoa powder
1/2 cup water
1 tablespoon cornstarch

To Make the Chocolate Cups: In a heavy saucepan, melt the chocolate over low heat and let cool slightly. Using a spoon or brush, coat the insides of four 9-ounce waxed paper cold-drink cups with a thin layer of chocolate, about halfway up. Refrigerate the cups until the chocolate is firm and repeat the coating process two more times, refrigerating for at least 30 minutes after the last coat. Carefully peel away the waxed paper cups and store the chocolate cups in the refrigerator until the filling is ready. The cups can be made ahead of time, if desired.

To Make the Filling: Press the ricotta cheese through a strainer into a large bowl. Sift the confectioners' sugar into the ricotta. Stir in the chocolate, cocoa powder, and vanilla until thoroughly combined.

To Make the Sauce: In a small saucepan, stir together the jam and sugar. Stir in the cocoa powder. In a small cup, stir together the water and cornstarch and add it to the jam mixture in the pan. Cook over medium heat, stirring constantly, until the mixture comes to a boil; let it boil, still stirring, until it is thick and smooth. Let cool.

To Assemble the Dessert: Fill each chocolate cup with some of the cheese mixture. Make a pool of raspberry sauce in the center of a dessert plate and position a filled cup in the center of the sauce.

Low-Cal Zabaglione

Makes 6 servings

H ere is a special sweet treat that has the health of your valentine's heart in mind. Chef Vincent Bommarito of Tony's in St. Louis developed this special recipe for "Live" with the express purpose of creating a dessert that was low in fat and calories but still tasted great. Zabaglione is a traditional Italian dessert that is made by whipping egg yolks with Marsala, sugar, and other ingredients into a frothy custard. In this version, the egg yolks are replaced by whipped, chilled skim milk. Yogurt is added for a thicker consistency, creating a dessert that is a fat-watcher's dream come true!

1/3 cup evaporated skim milk
6 cups mixed berries, washed and stemmed (such as
    raspberries, strawberries, and blackberries)
2 tablespoons low-fat vanilla yogurt
1 tablespoon Marsala
1 tablespoon sherry
1/4 teaspoon finely grated orange peel
1/4 teaspoon vanilla extract
2 tablespoons sifted confectioners' sugar

Place the evaporated skim milk in a medium bowl and cover with plastic wrap. Freeze for 30 minutes, or until ice crystals begin to form around the edge.

Arrange 1 cup of berries on each of six ovenproof dessert plates. Cover with plastic wrap and refrigerate.

Preheat the broiler of the oven and position the broiler so that it is 5 to 6 inches away from the heat source.

In a small bowl, whisk together the vanilla yogurt, Marsala, sherry, orange peel, and vanilla.

Using an electric mixer fitted with chilled beaters, beat the skim milk with the confectioners' sugar on high speed until the mixture forms soft peaks and has the consistency of whipped cream. Fold in the yogurt mixture just until it is combined.

Remove the plastic wrap from the chilled plates with the berries. Spoon about 1/3 cup of the whipped milk-yogurt mixture over the berries on each plate. Place the plates under the broiler and broil for about 1 minute, or just until each dessert is lightly browned on top. Serve immediately.

Chapter 4

Luck o' the Irish

..................~⚜~..................

S ituated on the calendar just before spring has sprung, at the time of the year when people are ready to chase away the winter blahs, St. Patrick's Day is a great time to have a party—even with your immediate family. March 17th is the feast day of St. Patrick, the patron saint of Ireland. St. Patrick was responsible for converting the pagan Irish to Christianity, and was also said to have driven all serpents and venomous creatures out of the land. Dishes celebrating St. Patrick's Day tend to be made from rustic basics, such as potatoes, lamb, cabbage, and stout. In the United States, green food coloring has come to play an important role; nowadays, you can see everything from green beer to emerald bagels.

This chapter is a collection of hearty recipes that will help your guests make it safely through those last cold days of winter. An Irish restaurateur, Eamonn Doran, shared his special recipe for a classic St. Patrick's Day recipe on "Live": Braised Irish Lamb Stew. Production assistant David Mullen offers his mom's recipe for Classic Irish Soda Bread. And last but not least, Kermit the Frog (who knows what being green is all about!) demonstrated his recipe for Shoofly Pie on the show, and it's here, too. A wedge of this pie is great with a big mug of Irish Coffee.

$\mathcal{M}$rs. $\mathcal{M}$ullen's $\mathcal{C}$lassic $\mathcal{I}$rish $\mathcal{S}$oda $\mathcal{B}$read

Makes 12 to 15 servings

Production assistant David Mullen brings this special bread into "Live" 's studio every St. Patrick's Day; he suggests including it in your own celebratory bread basket. It tastes especially good when spread with orange marmalade.

David says that one of the best parties he's ever been to was a New Year's Eve party hosted by a friend. Each room was given a different international food theme. For instance, the Mexican room served chips, salsa, and margaritas; the Japanese room had sushi and sake; and the Russian room was chilled by fans and had icicles hanging from the ceiling. Its signature beverage: a White Russian.

4 1/2 cups all-purpose flour
1 tablespoon plus 2 teaspoons baking powder
1 1/2 teaspoons salt
1/4 teaspoon baking soda
1 cup hydrogenated vegetable shortening, chilled
2 cups raisins
2 cups buttermilk
1/2 cup orange marmalade
2 large eggs, lightly beaten

Preheat the oven to 325°F. Grease a 10-inch cast iron skillet or a 3-quart casserole dish.

In a large bowl, stir together the flour, baking powder, salt, and baking soda until combined.

With a pastry blender or 2 knives used scissors fashion, cut in the shortening until the mixture resembles coarse crumbs. Stir in the raisins.

In another bowl, stir together the buttermilk, orange marmalade, and eggs until blended. Stir the buttermilk mixture into the flour mixture until combined. Scrape the mixture into the prepared pan and smooth the top. Bake for 70 to 80 minutes, or until the loaf is baked through.

Adding Irish Charm
to Your Party
~❦~

- Ask everyone to wear green. Those who don't are at risk of being pinched by everyone present.

- When you send out invitations, put "O'" in front of everyone's name and call them by this Irish moniker at the party—for instance, Mr. O'Steinberg and Ms. O'Capparelle. Use postcards from Ireland for your invitations, if there's a store near you that specializes in Irish items.

- Invest in a tape or CD of Irish folk songs to set the mood. Or go for popular music by Irish artists such as U2, The Cranberries, or Sinead O' Connor.

- Have a contest at the party for the best St. Patrick's Day limerick.

- Sensationalize an Irish staple by building a mountain of potatoes—brown, red, and purple—on your dining table or buffet table. For additional drama, place votive candles in clear glass holders in strategic spots on the mound. Continue the theme by serving hollowed-out new potatoes filled with sour cream sprinkled with caviar and chives as an hors d'oeuvre.

- Look for temporary shamrock tattoos for guests to wear.

- Decorate with the color green, and include at least one leprechaun for good luck.

- Make three round cake layers and fit them together to form a shamrock. Shape the pieces of cake that you cut from each layer to form the shamrock's stem. Ice the cake with green frosting.

- Serve crème de menthe liqueur or Irish cream liqueur over a scoop of vanilla ice cream in a stemmed glass as an easy and refreshing dessert. Make shamrock-shaped sugar cookies topped with green sprinkles as accompaniments.

Joanie's Hamburger-Barley Soup

Makes 10 to 12 servings

What could be better for entertaining than a soup that improves when it's made at least one day ahead of when you are going to serve it! The recipe also makes a generous quantity and freezes well. Joan Epstein, Kathie Lee's mother, prepared her original soup on a cold wintry day, to the delight of "Live"'s viewers. Fill insulated containers with this hearty soup for toting to ice-skating, sledding, or skiing parties.

1 tablespoon vegetable oil
2 pounds lean ground beef
7 cups water
1 can (16 ounces) whole tomatoes, chopped
3/4 cup tomato juice
1/2 pound fresh string beans, trimmed and cut into 1-inch
    pieces
1 green pepper, seeded and diced
1 cup diced celery
1/2 cup chopped celery leaves
1/2 cup pearl barley
2 tablespoons light soy sauce
2 teaspoons garlic powder
1 bay leaf
1/2 teaspoon paprika
1/2 teaspoon dried thyme leaves
Salt and pepper to taste
2 carrots, sliced
1 large potato, diced

In a large saucepot, heat the oil over medium heat. Add the ground beef and cook for about 10 minutes, or until the hamburger is thoroughly browned. Drain off the fat and discard.

Add the remaining ingredients except the carrots and potato. Bring the mixture to a boil, then reduce the heat, cover, and simmer for 1 hour. Add the carrots and cook for 10 minutes more. Add the potato and cook for 20 minutes longer. If necessary, add more water or tomato juice to achieve the desired consistency.

Shepherd's Pie

 This is the Love Chef's version of a classic recipe. For authenticity, serve it with a hearty stout.

1 pound ground beef
1 small onion, chopped
1 tablespoon olive oil (optional)
1 teaspoon Worcestershire sauce
1 cup fresh or thawed frozen peas
1 carrot, sliced and partially cooked
1 teaspoon dried sage leaves
1/2 teaspoon dried thyme leaves
Freshly ground black pepper to taste
Salt (optional)
3 potatoes, peeled, cooked, and mashed
1/4 cup (1/2 stick) unsalted (sweet) butter
Up to 1/2 cup milk

Preheat the oven to 375°F. Butter a 1 1/2-quart baking dish.

In a large skillet, cook the beef, onion, and olive oil, if using, over medium heat until lightly browned. Drain off the excess fat and discard. Stir in the Worcestershire sauce.

Place the beef mixture in the prepared baking dish. Add the peas and carrot. Sprinkle with the sage, thyme, pepper, and salt, if using it.

Mash the potatoes with 2 tablespoons of the butter and enough milk to make them the consistency you prefer. Taste and adjust the seasoning. Spread the mashed potatoes on top of the beef mixture and dot the top with small pieces of the remaining 2 tablespoons of butter. Bake for about 30 minutes, or until browned on top and heated through.

Note: This dish is traditionally made with leftover cooked lamb, hence the name Shepherd's Pie.

Braised Irish Lamb Stew

As the owner of three New York City Irish restaurants, Eamonn Doran was a natural choice for an appearance on "Live" to demonstrate a St. Patrick's Day recipe. Originally, lamb stew was a dish for poor people, but Eamonn's version is one you'll relish anytime you are looking for a comforting, filling meal. He recommends serving it with string beans flavored with strips of smoked bacon. In fact, that is the way he presented it on "Live," much to the dismay of Regis, who had just gotten doctor's orders to cut down his cholesterol intake. At the end of the segment, Eamonn presented Joy with an Irish potato made of crystal.

2 tablespoons vegetable oil
2 pounds neck, shoulder, or leg of lamb, cut into 1-inch
    pieces
2 large onions, diced
2 tomatoes, chopped
1 medium green or red bell pepper, seeded and chopped
    (optional)
1 garlic clove, crushed
1/2 teaspoon paprika
1/2 cup lamb stock or beef broth
Salt and pepper to taste
Chopped fresh parsley, for garnish
Freshly boiled potatoes

Preheat the oven to 350°F. In a large skillet, heat the oil over medium-high heat. Add the lamb and cook until it is browned on all sides. Using a slotted spoon, transfer the lamb to a shallow casserole dish.

Add the onions, tomatoes, bell pepper, if desired, garlic, and paprika to the skillet. Stir in the stock, salt, and pepper. Bring the mixture to a boil and pour it over the lamb in the casserole. Cover and bake for about 1 1/2 hours, or until the lamb is tender. Sprinkle with the parsley. Serve with freshly boiled potatoes.

Roast Chicken with Rosemary and Orange

Lidia Bastianich usually serves her mouthwatering northern Italian fare in her Felidia Ristorante in New York City. However, she took a break from its beautiful brownstone setting to come to "Live" and prepare this elegantly easy recipe for chicken from her book, *La Cucina di Lidia*. Lidia likes to serve this dish with the recipe that follows for gnocchi in a buttered vegetable sauce.

2 whole chickens (about 2 pounds each)
1/4 teaspoon salt
1/4 teaspoon ground pepper
3 tablespoons olive oil
6 tablespoons Grand Marnier
1/4 cup chicken stock or broth
3 tablespoons fresh orange juice
2 tablespoons fresh rosemary leaves
2 tablespoons brandy
2 tablespoons butter

Preheat the oven to 500°F.

Split the chickens down the back. Using a sharp paring knife and your fingers, cut out the backbones. Remove the breastbones and ribs. Combine the salt and pepper and sprinkle the mixture on both sides of each piece of chicken.

Heat a 14-inch ovenproof skillet over medium-high heat. Place the chickens skin side down in the skillet and cook for 5 minutes. Turn and brown for 5 minutes longer. Add the olive oil to the skillet.

Place the skillet in the preheated oven and roast for 30 minutes, turning the chickens occasionally. Remove the skillet from the oven and drain off all the fat.

(continued)

Add the remaining ingredients to the pan. Place the skillet over high heat and cook for 2 minutes, basting frequently and occasionally turning the chickens. Transfer the birds to warm serving plates and spoon the sauce in the pan over them.

How Do You Celebrate St. Patrick's Day?

~ ₹ ~

Regis: St. Paddy's Day is always a special day around "Live" as we always devote the whole show to its celebration. By the time I get through with the Irish toe dancers, the Irish singers, and the Irish chefs, that's our St. Patrick's Day celebration. The crowd usually comes in costume as they get ready for the big parade which begins right outside our doors. I always wear green on St. Patrick's Day. One year I didn't wear enough green—just a green tie, never enough for the Irish people in our audience—and I caught flack for that. Now I wear a green tie, green suit, and sometimes a green shirt. Our celebration of St. Patrick's Day is a major highlight once a year.

Kathie Lee: For St. Patrick's Day we usually celebrate at home, with a big corned beef and cabbage, and boiled potatoes. Or we go to Neary's, our favorite Irish pub in New York City, and celebrate with Jimmy Neary. He's the best Irishman I've ever known, the dearest man.

$\mathcal{G}$nocchi all'$\mathcal{O}$rtolana ($\mathcal{P}$otato $\mathcal{D}$umplings with a $\mathcal{G}$arden $\mathcal{S}$auce)

Makes 6 servings

L idia's classic recipe for the small potato dumplings called *gnocchi* smothers them deliciously with a buttery, fresh vegetable sauce. The gnocchi have small indentations that help them to cook more evenly and hold onto the sauce. Use your own favorite pasta sauce with these dumplings as a nice change of pace from regular pasta.

GNOCCHI

6 large Idaho or russet potatoes
2 tablespoons plus 1 teaspoon salt
2 large eggs, lightly beaten
Dash of freshly ground white pepper
3 to 4 cups unbleached all-purpose flour

FRESH VEGETABLE SAUCE

1 cup (2 sticks) unsalted (sweet) butter, cut into 1/2-inch
    pieces
4 fresh sage leaves
1 1/2 cups chicken stock or broth
1/2 cup fresh peas, steamed until just tender
1/2 cup cooked mixed beans and chickpeas
1/2 cup finely diced carrots, steamed until just tender
1/2 cup finely diced zucchini
1/2 cup fava beans, steamed
1/4 cup cooked lentils
Salt and freshly ground pepper to taste
Pinch of crushed red pepper flakes
Freshly grated Parmesan cheese, if desired

To Make the Gnocchi: In a large saucepot, combine the potatoes with enough water to cover them. Bring the water to a boil and continue boiling for about 40 minutes, or until the potatoes "give" easily when pierced with a skewer. Drain the potatoes and let cool.

When the potatoes are cool enough to handle, peel them and pass them through a ricer or press them through a colander. Spread the riced potatoes loosely on a baking sheet so that as much surface as possible is exposed to the air. Cool the potatoes completely.

In a large saucepot, bring 6 quarts of water and 2 tablespoons of the salt to a boil.

Meanwhile, on a cool, preferably marble work surface, gather the cold riced potatoes into a mound, forming a well in the center. In a small bowl, stir together the eggs, the remaining 1 teaspoon of salt, and the white pepper. Pour the mixture into the well. Work the potatoes and eggs together with both hands, gradually adding 2 to 3 cups of the flour, scraping up the dough from the work surface with a knife as often as necessary.

Dust the dough, your hands, and the work surface lightly with flour, and cut the dough into 6 equal parts. Continue to dust the dough, your hands, and the surface as long as the dough feels sticky.

Using both hands, roll each piece of dough into a rope about 1/2-inch thick. Cut the rope at 1/2-inch intervals. Indent each dumpling with your thumb, or use the tines of a fork to produce a ribbed effect.

A few at a time, drop the gnocchi into the boiling water, stirring gently and continuously with a wooden spoon. Cook for 2 to 3 minutes, or until they rise to the surface. Using a slotted spoon, remove the gnocchi from the water and transfer them to a warm platter, adding a little sauce, once you have prepared it. Continue cooking the gnocchi in batches until they are all cooked.

Meanwhile, make the Fresh Vegetable Sauce: In a large skillet, heat the butter and sage over low heat. Add the stock and the vegetables and season with the salt, pepper, and crushed red pepper flakes. Let simmer for about 5 minutes until heated through. Add the cooked gnocchi, turning them gently with a wooden spoon for 1 to 2 minutes, or until they are coated with the sauce and are heated through. Transfer the sauced gnocchi to serving plates and sprinkle with the grated Parmesan cheese and additional pepper, if desired. Serve immediately.

"She's not going to want me to hug her, is she?"

Ethel's Stuffed Cabbage

During "Family Cooking Week" Ethel Senese made this family favorite with the assistance of her sous-chef son-in-law, Regis. Michael Gelman, ever on his toes, was holding up a sign off-camera during the segment that said, "Be careful not to eat the toothpicks." When it was Kathie Lee's turn to sample the dish, she brought the sign out onto the set to show the audience.

Ethel recommends serving the savory cabbage on a cold, raw evening.

> 1 pound ground round
> 1/3 cup uncooked rice
> 1/3 cup chopped fresh parsley
> Salt and pepper to taste
> 1 small head cabbage
> 2 tablespoons vegetable oil
> 1/2 cup chopped onion
> 1 garlic clove, finely chopped
> 2 cans (16 ounces each) diced tomatoes, including juice
> 1 can (15 ounces) tomato sauce
> 1 teaspoon dried thyme leaves, crumbled
> 1 teaspoon dried basil leaves, crumbled
> 1/4 to 1/2 teaspoon granulated sugar

Bring a large pot of water to a boil.

Meanwhile, in a large bowl, stir together the meat, rice, parsley, salt, and pepper. Form the mixture into 8 balls and reserve.

Remove the core from the head of cabbage. Immerse the whole head in the boiling water until the leaves can be easily separated. Detach 8 large leaves from the stalk.

In a Dutch oven or large saucepot, heat the oil over medium heat. Add the onion and garlic and cook for 5 to 7 minutes, or until softened but not browned. Stir in the tomatoes, tomato sauce, thyme, basil, and sugar.

Place 1 of the meat-and-rice balls in the center of 1 of the softened cabbage leaves. Fold the sides in over the filling and secure them with a toothpick. Repeat with the remaining balls and leaves. Arrange the stuffed leaves, folded side down, in the liquid in the Dutch oven. Cover the pot and simmer for about 45 minutes, or until the stuffed leaves are cooked through.

World Balancing Champion John Evans gives Regis a lift from the loading zone.

Kermit the Frog's
Shoofly Pie for Humans

Kermit the Frog made a special guest appearance on "Live" to promote his book *One Frog Can Make a Difference: Kermit's Guide to Life in the '90s*. When Kermit was asked why he had selected the following recipe to demonstrate, he said, "Well, um, we picked Shoofly Pie because we thought it was the easiest of the recipes to convert from swamp to studio cuisine. Usually it is served with lots of green flies dotting the top of the pie (actually, it serves as a fly-catcher). Since we left them out of the human version I still think you're missing a lot of the taste, but they didn't want any flies on the show." While we're sure Kermit's family enjoys the frog version, we're quite honestly glad he prepared the human version for us!

1 cup dark molasses
1/2 cup hot water
2 large eggs, lightly beaten
1 1/4 cups self-rising cake flour
2 teaspoons ground cinnamon
1/2 teaspoon ground nutmeg
1/2 teaspoon ground ginger
1/3 cup unsalted (sweet) butter, chilled
3/4 cup raisins
1 unbaked 9-inch pie shell

Preheat the oven to 450°F.

In a large bowl, stir together the molasses, water, and eggs. In another bowl, stir together the flour, cinnamon, nutmeg, and ginger. Using a pastry blender or 2 knives used scissors fashion, cut in the butter until the mixture resembles coarse crumbs.

Place most of the raisins in the bottom of the pie shell. Sprinkle about one-third of the flour mixture over the raisins. Top with about half of the molasses mixture. Sprinkle another layer of flour, top with the rest of the molasses mixture, and end with a layer of the flour mixture sprinkled evenly over the top of the molasses mixture. Sprinkle the remaining raisins over the top of the pie. Bake for 10 minutes at 450°F. Then reduce the heat to 350°F. and bake for 20 to 25 minutes longer, or until the top is fairly firm.

Learning How to Entertain
~ꝋ~

Kathie Lee: When I was growing up, it was a big deal for a teenager to have parties in the backyard, but my parents never let us do that. My mother said, "What I will do is let you have luncheons or dinner parties, and you will cook the food and set the table and pick the flowers."

She taught me how to entertain in a gracious way rather than to have a bunch of people over for pretzels and chips. She taught me the importance of presenting a beautiful table, and planning a menu and a schedule of the evening's activities. I'm very grateful to her for that, because it required her involvement. It would have been easier for her and my father to have said, "Sure, have all your friends over, put them in the backyard, and we'll split for the evening." But they never allowed that. They said, "No, if you can't learn something from it, then you're not going to do it." I think that was very wise of them.

Chapter 5

April Showers

·················· ∽❦∽ ··················

e gave this chapter its name because it celebrates spring and also because the recipes in this chapter are ideal for showers—both for brides and babies. These days, showers aren't just for the ladies anymore, and you might want to invite couples; men are sure to like Tommy Tang's 'Nam Chicken appetizer. Chef Tell's Mediterranean-style Roast Chicken is served with orzo, small, rice-shaped pasta that is tossed with tangy feta cheese. His recipe for Vegetable Tarts is a pleasing accompaniment. Maria DiSaverio serves up Penne with Shrimp and Asparagus, a delightful pasta recipe that takes advantage of asparagus being at its peak. Of course, these celebratory recipes are great for any springtime party.

What is the most memorable party you have ever been to?

~❦~

Regis: Malcolm Forbes's seventieth birthday party in Morocco in August, 1990. It was the most fabulous party anyone has ever thrown. We were flown to Morocco along with some of the most influential and famous people in the country. Malcolm chartered three big jets for the trip. He renovated and air-conditioned a whole hotel, and he did everything he could to make his guests comfortable. We spent about four days there. It was an unforgettable experience. There will never be another party like it—sightseeing all over Tangiers, haggling with the shopkeepers in the Casbah—and it all climaxed with his sensational birthday party held under five different tents at his palace overlooking the Mediterranean. Elizabeth Taylor was the hostess, and opera star Beverly Sills sang "Happy Birthday" to Malcolm. No one who was there will ever forget it.

How did you get on that list?

~❦~

Regis: We met when he guested on my TV show. We became friends and he introduced Joy and me to so many interesting people and places. We spent many fabulous nights on his yacht, *The Highlander.* We were there for Liz Taylor's birthday party at his New Jersey estate, and you should have seen the helicopters lined up on the fields outside his home. We spent a memorable weekend at his château in France, ballooned with him over the French vineyards, flew back and forth in his jet. He was a great host and great gentleman. He had style and flair and always made you feel like you were his most important guest. He was a great New York character, lived life to the fullest, and was a wonderful inspiration. I can't tell you how much we miss him.

Showering Your Guests with Attention

~❦~

- Set out small pots with spring-flowering bulbs at each place setting. Tie color-coordinating bows on each pot.

- Continue the theme with flowers made out of food. Place grilled shrimp in a circle as "petals"; a grilled scallion, including the white bulb, as the "stem and roots"; brown rice as the "soil." Finish with a scoop of ice cream in a small flower pot lined with a muffin cup and topped with edible flowers.

- Give out umbrellas as party favors and use miniature umbrellas to decorate the beverages.

- If it's a bridal shower, decorate in the bride's colors; if it's a baby shower, decorate in the colors of the rainbow, or in pastels.

- Ask guests to bring gifts in an "around-the-clock" theme, assigning each guest a specific time of day or night. This will help to encourage conversation as the gifts are opened.

- Collect attractive single-serving bottled water containers of pale green, cobalt blue, and clear glass. Place one or two single spring blooms in each. Cluster them for a seasonal centerpiece, or separate them and add one to each place setting.

- Fill a wooden box with small herb plants as a centerpiece. Give the plants to the guests as they depart.

- Hosting a bridal shower? Send each guest a blank scrapbook page and ask each one to create a personal message for the guest of honor, including photos, memorabilia, poetry, and the like. Assemble the pages as they are returned and, at the shower, present the bride-to-be with an album filled with memories and good wishes.

- For a baby shower, you could fold the napkins to look like diapers.

- Play a tape of birdsong or sea chanteys to heighten the guests' enjoyment of the season.

If you could have any three people to a dinner party at your house, who would they be?

≈☙≈

Regis: Barbara Walters, Jack Paar, and Charles Grodin, and, of course, my good friend Bobby DeNiro.

Kathie Lee: Frank, Cody, and Cassidy, and Frank would cook. We'd probably have my mother's spaghetti. That's about the best thing in the world. We'd all be smeared with spaghetti sauce. Cody likes to eat his spaghetti the way that Lady and the Tramp eat spaghetti, so it gets a little messy—but it's worth the clean-up.

Francis Anthony, the Love Chef, talks up the tastiness of his Halloween dish, but Regis's face tells a different story.

Mediterranean-style Roast Chicken

Makes 4 to 6 servings

Orzo is a small, rice-shaped pasta that Chef Tell uses in a recipe that captures the sunny flavor of the Mediterranean. Offer an interesting assortment of olives as an accompaniment to this main dish, along with a crisp green salad and some crusty bread. Serve cruets of olive oil and balsamic vinegar and invite guests to pour little pools of each onto their bread plates and dip the bread into them.

1 3-pound roasting chicken, cut into pieces
Juice of 2 lemons
20 garlic cloves, peeled
Fresh or dried oregano leaves
Salt and pepper to taste
1/2 cup olive oil
6 cups cooked orzo
1/2 cup crumbled feta or Romano cheese

Place the chicken pieces in a shallow glass baking dish. Pour the lemon juice over the chicken, cover, and refrigerate overnight.

Using the point of a sharp knife, make slits in the chicken. Insert the garlic cloves and oregano into the slits. Cover, and refrigerate for 2 to 4 hours longer.

Preheat the oven to 375°F. Season the chicken with additional oregano, salt, and pepper. Rub the chicken with the olive oil. Bake for about 1 hour and 20 minutes, or until the chicken is cooked through, turning occasionally.

During the last 20 minutes of baking, heat the orzo in a baking dish. Sprinkle the cheese over the top. When the chicken is cooked, pour the liquid in the baking dish over the orzo and serve it with the chicken.

Tommy Tang's 'Nam Chicken

Restauranteur Tommy Tang prepared this Vietnamese appetizer along with the recommendation that "spicy food is good for better loving." As Regis sampled the food after Tommy's demonstration, he said, "Let's eat this so we can be better lovers!" Tommy has namesake restaurants in Los Angeles.

You can use shrimp or fish in place of the chicken in this low-fat recipe, which also makes a superb luncheon main course.

2 tablespoons chicken stock or broth
6 ounces chicken breast, finely chopped
1/4 cup finely chopped unsalted dry roasted peanuts
1/4 cup sliced red onion
3 tablespoons finely chopped scallions
2 tablespoons finely chopped fresh gingerroot
2 tablespoons chopped fresh coriander leaves
1 tablespoon Thai fish sauce
1 tablespoon freshly squeezed lime juice
1 teaspoon finely chopped garlic
1/2 teaspoon cayenne pepper
Chopped red bell pepper, for garnish (optional)
About 10 lettuce leaves, washed and patted dry

In a medium skillet, heat the chicken stock over medium heat for 1 minute. Stir in the chicken and cook and stir for 2 to 3 minutes, or until the chicken is cooked and the stock has nearly evaporated.

Remove the skillet from the heat and stir in the remaining ingredients except the optional red bell pepper and the lettuce leaves.

Mound the mixture in the center of a platter and sprinkle with chopped red bell pepper, if desired. Surround the mixture with the lettuce leaves.

To serve, spoon small mounds of the mixture onto individual lettuce leaves and fold each leaf around the mixture.

What Is Fish Sauce, Anyway?

~❦~

Soy sauce is extremely popular in China and Japan, but in Southeast Asia, fish sauce is the flavoring and dipping sauce of choice. Fish sauces, made from unsalted and fermented fish, were first used in the western world by the ancient Romans. They liked to flavor their food with anchovy sauces.

Fish sauce is made by salting down small fish that are packed in wooden barrels. The liquid that collects is cooked and bottled. The aroma of fish sauce, similar to some strong-smelling cheeses, is much more pungent than the taste. And like the cheeses, the flavor of fish sauces is worth getting used to.

Shower Talk

~❦~

Kathie Lee: Eva Mohr, my good friend who is Cody's godmother, gave me a baby shower for Cody. She also gave me a wedding shower right before I was married. And then my dear friend Pat George, who was the beauty editor at "Good Morning America" when I was there, gave me a beautiful shower in her apartment in New York. And my wonderful friend Annie Siegel gave me a huge shower, and everybody I know was invited to that one. It was very lavish. She had Robert Isabelle do the flowers and they were unbelievable. That one was held in a private room at the 21 Club. Diane Sawyer, Helen Gurley Brown, and Phyllis George were there. It was a star-studded event. I couldn't believe it was for me.

Caribbean Chicken Drums

Makes 4 servings

If April's showers are getting you down, take a taste trip to the tropics with this main course from Rosemarie Berger of North Carolina, which won first prize at the 40th National Chicken Cooking Contest in 1993. In addition to a prize of $25,000, Rosemarie also won the opportunity to appear on "Live" with Regis as her sous-chef. Rosemarie was experimenting with Caribbean flavors as she developed this recipe, and the name Caribbean Drums came into her mind; that is why she used drumsticks, she reports: "Other parts could be used, but the drums are really *unbeatable!*"

She likes to serve this dish with couscous, and a tossed green salad with a vinegar and oil dressing. You could add a little grated lemon peel to the dressing, and include other tropical additions to the salad, such as marinated hearts of palm, avocado, and orange sections. Dessert can be as simple as lime sherbet or crackers served with a mild cheese, such as Monterey Jack or cream cheese, topped with guava jelly or guava paste.

Spring is carnival time in Jamaica and Rosemarie suggests that April is an ideal month for hosting a Caribbean party. "Set the mood with brightly colored tablecloths and napkins," she says. "Decorate with tropical plants and flowers. Set out baskets of tropical fruits, such as bananas, mangoes, papayas, kiwis, starfruits, oranges, and so on. Don't forget to play calypso music in the background—and how about a limbo contest?"

With this imaginative recipe and these great party suggestions, it's not surprising that Rosemarie won this cooking contest!

2 tablespoons vegetable oil
8 broiler-fryer chicken drumsticks
1 can (14 1/2 ounces) whole peeled tomatoes, cut into
   chunks

1 can (4 ounces) diced green chilies
1 tablespoon firmly packed brown sugar
1/4 teaspoon ground allspice
1/4 cup mango chutney, chopped
1/4 cup dark seedless raisins
1 tablespoon freshly squeezed lemon juice
1 large banana, sliced
1 ripe mango, sliced

In a large skillet, heat the oil over medium heat. Add the chicken and cook, turning occasionally, for about 10 minutes, or until brown on all sides.

Add the tomatoes, chilies, brown sugar, and allspice. Bring the mixture to a boil, then cover, reduce the heat to low, and cook for 20 minutes. Add the chutney, raisins, and lemon juice. Cover, and cook for about 15 minutes, or until a fork can be inserted in the chicken with ease.

Transfer the chicken to a serving platter. Using a spoon, skim the fat off the sauce. Add the banana to the mixture in the skillet and heat thoroughly.

Spoon the fruit and a little of the sauce over the chicken. Garnish with the mango slices. Place the remaining sauce in a separate dish and serve it with the chicken.

Penne with Shrimp and Asparagus

Makes 4 servings

Maria DiSaverio, owner of the Manhattan restaurant Tre Scalini, prepared a recipe that elegantly showcases the first tender asparagus of spring. She selected this recipe because it is a meal in itself, containing carbohydrate, protein, and vegetables. To accompany it, Maria recommends a refreshing salad made of oranges tossed with olive oil, a touch of vinegar, and a dash of oregano. During Maria's demonstration, Joy Philbin turned to Regis and commented that Maria reminded her of Regis's mother. Regis's response: "Maybe yes, but in a younger version."

14 ounces asparagus
16 large shrimp
16 ounces penne pasta
1/2 cup olive oil, divided
4 garlic cloves, finely chopped, divided
4 plum tomatoes, diced
1/2 cup white wine
Salt and pepper to taste

Snap off the stems of the asparagus at the point where they break naturally. If the asparagus is woody, peel the stems with a vegetable peeler or sharp knife. Bring some water to a boil in a large, deep skillet. Add the asparagus spears and cook for 1 to 2 minutes, or just until they are tender. Remove the asparagus from the skillet and cut each spear into 1/4-inch pieces, separating the tender tip pieces from the stem pieces.

Peel and devein the shrimp. To devein the shrimp, using the point of a sharp knife, make a shallow cut down the center back (the curved side) of each shrimp and remove the dark vein. Rinse away any bits of the vein that remain.

Bring a large pot of salted water to a boil. Add the penne and cook just until *al dente*. Drain thoroughly.

In a large pan, heat 1/4 cup of the olive oil over medium-high heat. Cook 3 of the garlic cloves for 1 to 2 minutes, or until golden. Add the pieces of asparagus stems and cook 2 minutes longer. Add the pieces of asparagus tips and the tomatoes and stir over low heat for 2 minutes.

In another skillet, heat the remaining 1/4 cup of oil over medium-high heat. Cook the remaining garlic clove for 1 to 2 minutes, or until golden. Add the shrimp and cook for 2 minutes. Stir in the wine, salt, and pepper and cook until about three-fourths of the wine has evaporated. Stir the shrimp mixture into the asparagus mixture. Add the cooked penne and toss to combine. Serve immediately.

All About Asparagus

While asparagus, a member of the lily family, is now available almost all year from sources around the world, American-grown asparagus is one of the first signs of spring. The tenderness of asparagus is a matter of age, not diameter. The younger the asparagus, the more tender it is. The spears should have tightly closed buds. Always store asparagus in the refrigerator. Some authorities recommend treating the spears as you would fresh flowers: Break off the tough ends and stand the spears upright in water.

Early Egyptians are said to have enjoyed the delights of wild asparagus before the second pyramid was constructed. Certainly, the ancient Greeks and Romans prized asparagus both as a food and as medicine. Several cultures have attributed aphrodisiacal powers to the plant. In 19th-century France, in fact, a bridegroom's prenuptial dinner consisted of at least three courses of warm asparagus!

Vegetable Couscous with Lamb

Makes 6 servings

 When Regis and Kathie Lee paid a visit to Walt Disney World, the show featured foods prepared with international flair. One of their guest chefs was Lahsen Abrache, executive chef of the Restaurant Marrakesh in EPCOT Center. Lahsen selected the following recipe to demonstrate because it is a signature Moroccan recipe that is extremely popular in his restaurant. He emphasized the importance of presenting the dish attractively—presentation is a major element in all Moroccan food. To give the dish extra flavor, the liquid from cooking the lamb is used to prepare the couscous.

2 pounds of lamb leg or shoulder, trimmed of visible fat and
  cut into 2-inch cubes
1 onion, sliced
1 bunch fresh coriander leaves, chopped
2 tablespoons olive oil, divided
1 tablespoon salt
1 teaspoon ground pepper
Pinch of saffron
Pinch of turmeric
1/2 pound carrots, cut into 1/2-by-3-inch strips
1/2 pound turnips, cut into 1/2-by-3-inch strips
1/2 pound zucchini, cut into 1/2-by-3-inch strips
1/2 pound cherry tomatoes
1/2 pound cooked or canned drained chickpeas
2 tablespoons raisins
1 box (12 ounces) couscous

In a very large saucepot, bring 1 gallon of water to a boil. Add the lamb, onion, coriander, 1 1/2 tablespoons of the olive oil, salt, pepper, saffron, and turmeric. Let the mixture return to a boil, then reduce the heat, and simmer uncovered for 1 hour.

Add the vegetables, chickpeas, and raisins and cook for 30 minutes more.

Prepare the couscous according to the package directions, using some of the broth from the lamb mixture. Drizzle the prepared couscous with the remaining 1/2 tablespoon of olive oil and toss gently to combine.

To serve, spread the couscous on the plate and place the lamb cubes in the center. Arrange the vegetables and chickpeas attractively on the top. Pour enough of the lamb broth over everything to moisten it and sprinkle the top with the raisins.

Entertaining, Moroccan Style

~❦~

To create a dining experience with Moroccan flair, here are a few tips from Lahsen Abrache:

- Make sure every dish is presented in a fashion worthy of a feast.

- Start the meal with a "milk and date" ceremony. In Morocco, this ceremony is used to welcome special guests. Each guest must take one date and one sip of milk—never more.

- Before you begin to eat, offer each guest a warm hand towel that has been moistened and perhaps perfumed with a little fragrance, such as orange blossom.

- At the end of the meal, sprinkle each guest's hands with orange-blossom water. In Morocco, a daughter of the family is usually in charge of this ceremony. For fun, she sometimes splashes the hair and nape of the neck of one or more guests.

Spring Bada-Bing Lamb Chops

Makes 4 servings

I t seems that whenever The Clever Cleaver Brothers come to visit New York from their home in San Diego, it rains. That's why this recipe is in the April Showers chapter.

For the segment in which this recipe was introduced, a big grill was set up outside the WABC studio. "Live" 's crew had decorated it with all sorts of beachy gear in honor of The Clever Cleaver Brothers' arrival. And still it drizzled and drizzled.

However, the rain didn't dampen the spirits of the ever-enthusiastic Clever Cleavers. Leeza Gibbons was pinch-hitting for Kathie Lee, and Robert Pastorelli from "Murphy Brown" was a walk-on guest. As Regis, Leeza, and Robert sampled the recipe, The Clever Cleaver Brothers, dressed in tank tops and loud shorts, kept everyone dry with a beach umbrella.

1 cup olive oil
1/2 cup red wine
1/4 cup chopped fresh mint leaves
1 tablespoon freshly squeezed lemon juice
1 garlic clove, finely chopped
Few dashes of Angostura low-sodium Worcestershire sauce
4 large lamb chops

In a shallow glass dish, mix together the oil, wine, mint, lemon juice, garlic, and Worcestershire sauce. (You can mix the marinade ingredients together the day before and store the marinade in the refrigerator.) Add the lamb chops, cover, and refrigerate for at least 2 hours, turning the chops occasionally.

Using a paper towel, lightly rub a little vegetable oil on the grill or broiler pan. Position the grill or broiler 5 to 6 inches away from the heat source and cook the chops for approximately 5 minutes on each side, or until they are done to your taste. Remove the chops and serve with your favorite barbecue items.

Vegetable Tarts

 or his 1990 Earth Day appearance, Chef Tell demonstrated these individual free-form tarts, which use a variety of vegetables from our planet Earth. For a firsthand taste of Chef Tell's cuisine, visit Chef Tell's Grand Old House in the Cayman Islands and Chef Tell's Harrow Inne in Ottsville, Pennsylvania.

1 cup olive oil, divided
10 garlic cloves, mashed
2 eggplants, peeled and cut into 1/2-inch-thick slices
2 zucchini squash, cut into 1/4-inch-thick slices
2 yellow squash, cut into 1/4-inch-thick slices
12 slices fresh tomato
6 to 8 fresh basil leaves, chopped
About 1/4 cup chopped fresh parsley
Salt and pepper to taste
1 cup chopped peeled, seeded tomatoes
Chervil to taste

Preheat the oven to 375°F.

In a large skillet, heat 1/2 cup of the oil and 6 of the garlic cloves over medium heat. Add the eggplant, zucchini, and yellow squash. Cook for 7 to 10 minutes, or until softened slightly. Remove the vegetables to several layers of paper towels and drain thoroughly.

Layer the vegetables in 4 rounded stacks on a baking sheet. Top with the tomato slices. Sprinkle with half of the basil, the parsley, salt, and pepper. Bake for 25 minutes.

Meanwhile, in the container of a blender or food processor, process the chopped tomatoes. Gradually add the remaining 1/2 cup of oil and the remaining 4 garlic cloves. Season to taste with the chervil, the remaining basil, salt, and pepper. Spoon the tomato mixture evenly onto 4 individual plates. Place a vegetable "tart" on top of each plate.

Edible Flowers

~❦~

- Nasturtiums bloom in colors varying from white to orange to deep red. With their pungent, peppery flavor, the flowers (and leaves) are a terrific addition to salads.

- Rose petals can be floated in white wine or added to a bowl of spring greens for a delicate flavor.

- Violets and pansies add a colorful dash to canapés. Candied violets are a pretty decoration for desserts.

Kathie Lee lets Gelman sample some pasta.

$\mathcal{KFC}$
($\mathcal{K}$entucky $\mathcal{F}$ried $\mathcal{C}$hicken)
$\mathcal{C}$oleslaw

Cookbook author Tod Wilbur dedicated five years to duplicating the exact taste of some of America's favorite store-bought foods, and published the results of his labors in his book, *Top-Secret Recipes*. Any one of the following four recipes would be great as April Fool's Day fare.

On "Live," Todd demonstrated the recipe for his interpretation of KFC (Kentucky Fried Chicken) Coleslaw and he recommends serving it with KFC Chicken and KFC Biscuits (his recipes follow). For a "real" KFC experience, use paper plates and plastic utensils.

Note: Todd says that, when chopping the cabbage and carrots for the coleslaw, it is important that they be cut into very small pieces, about the size of rice kernels.

1/2 cup mayonnaise
1/3 cup granulated sugar
1/4 cup buttermilk
1/4 cup milk
2 1/2 tablespoons lemon juice
1 1/2 tablespoons white vinegar
1/2 teaspoon salt
1/8 teaspoon ground pepper
8 cups very finely chopped cabbage (1 medium head)
1/4 cup very finely shredded carrot (1 medium carrot)

In a large bowl, stir together all of the ingredients except the cabbage and carrot until the mixture is smooth.

Add the cabbage and carrot and mix well. Cover and refrigerate for at least 2 hours before serving. (Todd reports that the critical part of this recipe is the flavor-enhancement period prior to eating. Make sure that you allow enough time for the coleslaw to refrigerate for at least 2 hours.)

$\mathcal{KFC}\ O_{riginal}\ \mathcal{R}_{ecipe}$ $\mathcal{F}_{ried}\ C_{hicken}$

Makes 12 pieces of chicken

 Here is Todd's interpretation of one of America's favorite take-out foods; again, the recipe is from his book, *Top-Secret Recipes*. Todd reports that Colonel Sanders discovered that a pressure cooker is quicker than a skillet for frying chicken (10 minutes), and that the process keeps the chicken moist and juicy inside.

6 cups Crisco cooking oil
2 cups milk
1 large egg, beaten
2 cups all-purpose flour
1/4 cup salt
2 teaspoons ground black pepper
1 teaspoon MSG (monosodium glutamate; or you can use Accent Flavor Enhancer)
2 frying chickens with skin, each cut into 6 pieces

Pour the oil into the pressure cooker and heat over medium heat to about 400°F.

In a small bowl, combine the milk and egg.

In another bowl or on a flat plate, stir together the flour, salt, pepper, and MSG.

Dip each piece of chicken in the milk mixture until it is moistened all over. Roll the moistened chicken in the flour mixture until it is completely coated.

In groups of four or five, drop the flour-covered chicken pieces into the oil and lock the pressure-cooker lid in place.

When steam begins shooting through the pressure release, set the time for 10 minutes.

After 10 minutes, release the pressure according to the manufacturer's instructions. Remove the chicken to paper towels or a metal rack to drain. Keep warm, while you repeat the process with the remaining chicken.

KFC Buttermilk Biscuits

 Todd worked diligently to produce this clone of the highly acclaimed recipe for KFC's Buttermilk Biscuits.

5 cups Bisquick biscuit mix
3/4 cup buttermilk
1/2 cup (1 stick) unsalted (sweet) butter, softened
1/4 cup club soda
1 large egg, beaten
2 1/2 tablespoons granulated sugar
1 teaspoon salt

Preheat the oven to 450°F. Butter a baking sheet.

In a large bowl, stir together all of the ingredients. Knead the dough by hand until smooth.

Flour your hands. On waxed paper, pat the dough flat to a 3/4-inch thickness. Cut out biscuits with a 2- to 3-inch-diameter biscuit cutter. Place the biscuits on the prepared baking sheet. Bake for 12 minutes, or until golden brown.

McDonald's Big Mac

Regis sampled Todd's version of a Big Mac on "Live" and said it tasted just like the original. Here's the recipe so that you can do your own taste testing.

1 sesame seed hamburger bun plus half of an additional
   hamburger bun
1/4 pound ground beef
Dash of salt
1 tablespoon Kraft Thousand Island dressing
1 teaspoon finely diced onion
1/2 cup chopped iceberg lettuce
1 slice American cheese
2 to 3 dill pickle slices

With a serrated knife, cut off the top of the extra bun half, leaving a slice about 3/4 inch thick. This will be the middle bun in your sandwich.

Place the three bun halves on a hot skillet or griddle, face down, and toast them to a light brown. Set aside the bun halves, but keep the skillet hot.

Divide the ground beef in half and press each half into a thin patty that is slightly larger than the bun.

Cook the patties in the hot skillet over medium heat for 2 to 3 minutes on each side. Salt lightly.

Build the burger in the following stacking order from the bottom up:

1. Bottom bun
2. Half of dressing
3. Half of onion
4. Half of lettuce
5. American cheese
6. Beef patty
7. Middle bun
8. Remainder of dressing
9. Remainder of onion
10. Remainder of lettuce
11. Pickle slices
12. Beef patty
13. Top bun

Chapter 6

Happy Easter and Passover Recipes with Panache

······· ~❦~ ·······

F or many people, Easter and Passover are filled with religious traditions; these holidays are also two of our favorite times for getting together with friends and family for celebration and feasting. There are recipes in this chapter for meals that celebrate the holidays for both religious persuasions. In fact, we think it is an honor to be invited to share and learn about the special holidays that each of us celebrates.

Chef Tell's Scotch Leg of Lamb is a great choice not only at Easter but at any springtime meal. For dessert, try Father Joseph Orsini's out-of-the-ordinary Easter cheesecake.

Potatoes play an important part in many Jewish meals. On "Live," cookbook author Joan Nathan shared her special recipe for Passover Potato Pudding and actor Freddie Roman demonstrated his Mother-in-Law's Potato Pancakes. Either of these recipes would be equally suitable as a side dish, whatever the time of year.

What do you eat for Easter?

Regis: Joy usually makes ham and scalloped potatoes with all the side dishes, but for the past several years the whole family has accompanied me to Walt Disney World for the holiday because I host the Easter Parade with Joan Lunden.

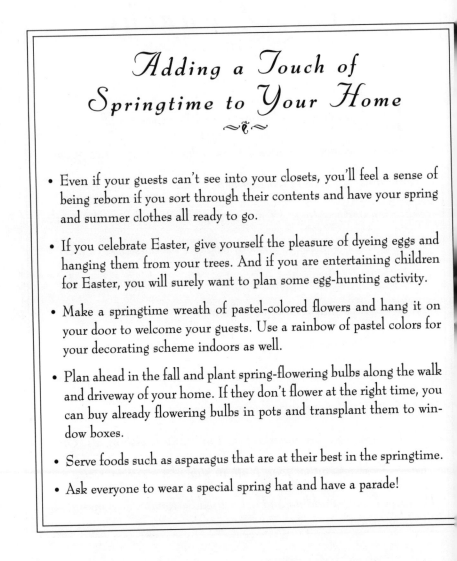

Adding a Touch of Springtime to Your Home

- Even if your guests can't see into your closets, you'll feel a sense of being reborn if you sort through their contents and have your spring and summer clothes all ready to go.

- If you celebrate Easter, give yourself the pleasure of dyeing eggs and hanging them from your trees. And if you are entertaining children for Easter, you will surely want to plan some egg-hunting activity.

- Make a springtime wreath of pastel-colored flowers and hang it on your door to welcome your guests. Use a rainbow of pastel colors for your decorating scheme indoors as well.

- Plan ahead in the fall and plant spring-flowering bulbs along the walk and driveway of your home. If they don't flower at the right time, you can buy already flowering bulbs in pots and transplant them to window boxes.

- Serve foods such as asparagus that are at their best in the springtime.

- Ask everyone to wear a special spring hat and have a parade!

Scotch Leg of Lamb

Chef Tell comes to the rescue with this splendid version of a springtime classic—just what you want for serving at an Easter family get-together.

3 carrots
3 celery stalks
2 turnips
2 to 3 garlic cloves
Salt and pepper to taste
7- to 8-pound leg of lamb
2 to 3 tablespoons vegetable oil
1 onion, chopped
1 to 2 cups water or stock

Cut 2 of the carrots into approximately 20 thin strips. Cut 2 of the stalks of celery into approximately 20 thin strips. Cut the turnips into approximately 20 thin strips. Cut the garlic cloves into slivers.

Using the point of a sharp knife, make slits in the leg of lamb. Insert the vegetable strips and the garlic into the slits. Season the lamb with salt and pepper.

Preheat the oven to 375°F.

In a very large skillet, heat the oil over medium-high heat. Brown the leg of lamb on all sides. Remove the lamb from the pan and place it in a large roasting pan. Insert a meat thermometer into the center of the thickest part of the meat, taking care not to touch the bone. Roast for 45 minutes.

Meanwhile, chop the remaining carrot and the remaining celery stalk and add them to the oil in the skillet. Add the onion and cook over medium-high heat for 7 to 10 minutes, or until all the vegetables are softened slightly. Add the vegetables to the roasting pan and continue roasting for 45 to 60 minutes longer, or until the lamb has reached the desired degree of doneness, 140°F., for rare, 160°F. for medium, or 170°F. for well done.

Transfer the lamb to a serving platter and keep it warm.

To Make a Sauce: Place the roasting pan on a burner over medium heat. Add the water or stock to the pan and, using a wooden spoon, scrape the pan to loosen the vegetables from the bottom. (This is called deglazing the pan.)

Slice the lamb and arrange the slices on a warm serving platter. Pour the sauce over the meat.

$\mathcal{M}$emories of $\mathcal{F}$amily $\mathcal{P}$arties
~ℓ~

Regis: When I was growing up, our parties were always family style. We lived with my grandmother and my uncle, and the rest of the family lived upstairs from us, so there was a lot of dining with relatives.

My mother was a terrific cook and she made a lot of great Italian dishes, plus steaks and hams. People in those days seemed to enjoy food a little more than they do now. Everybody's so weight-conscious and calorie-conscious these days.

We still have family reunions. In fact, we just had one. It was a simple Saturday afternoon lunch with deli-type sandwiches and side dishes. The fact that it was a no-fuss lunch made it more fun, and we had more time for reminiscing.

Kathie Lee: My childhood birthdays were always kind of disappointing because my birthday is August 16th, and we were always out of school then. Everybody who had their birthdays during the school year got a party, and presents from their friends. My birthdays were always on the lonely side, because everybody was gone for the summer.

My family would try to make it fun for me, but it was usually just a family event, usually at Rehoboth Beach, because that's where my mom and dad run an inn. So I don't really have any memories of big, big parties. It was a busy time of the year for the whole family. We were working.

Carrot S oufflé

Makes 6 servings

Segment producer Rosemary Kalikow enjoys cooking on the weekends, when she has more time. Her Saturday-night meals are a little more elaborate than those she prepares during the week. This carrot recipe is even a hit with her seven-year-old son, Brett (and it's a great way to get him to eat vegetables). When Rosemary entertains, she likes to have lots of fresh flowers around the house, and for extra-special parties she adds a little live music.

SOUFFLÉ
1 pound cooked sliced carrots
3 large eggs or 4 large egg whites
1/2 cup (1 stick) unsalted (sweet) butter, melted
1/3 cup granulated sugar
3 tablespoons all-purpose flour
1 teaspoon vanilla extract
Pinch of ground nutmeg

TOPPING (OPTIONAL)
3 tablespoons firmly packed brown sugar
2 teaspoons unsalted (sweet) butter, softened
1/3 cup crushed cornflakes

Preheat the oven to 350°F.

To Make the Soufflé: In the container of a blender or a food processor fitted with the metal chopping blade, process the carrots and eggs until smooth. Add the remaining soufflé ingredients and process until combined.

Pour the mixture into a 1 1/2-quart baking dish. Bake for 50 to 60 minutes. If desired, in a small bowl, stir together the topping ingredients and sprinkle the mixture over the top. Bake 10 minutes longer, or until the soufflé is set and lightly browned on top. Serve immediately.

Priest and cookbook author Father Joseph Orsini demonstrated this dense and delicious Italian-style cheesecake on "Live." "Pastera" is a pie traditionally made in Italy for the celebration of Easter. The wheat berries give the pie a unique texture. Father Orsini recommends serving it with cups of espresso as a fitting finale to your Easter dinner.

1/2 pound (1/4 cup) wheat berries (available in health food
    stores and Italian specialty stores)
3/4 cup water
2 uncooked pie crusts (9 inches each)
1 3/4 pounds (3 cups) ricotta cheese
3/4 cup granulated sugar
3 large eggs
1 1/2 teaspoons ground cinnamon
1 1/2 teaspoons vanilla extract
1/4 teaspoon salt
1/4 cup chopped candied citrus peel
1 tablespoon melted butter
Confectioners' sugar for dusting the top

In a small bowl, soak the wheat berries in the water overnight. Drain, reserving the soaking liquid. Measure the liquid and add more water to make 3/4 cup. In a small saucepan, bring the wheat berries and the liquid to a boil. Reduce the heat to medium-low and simmer for about 50 minutes, or until the berries are tender. Drain and cool completely.

Preheat the oven to 350°F. Roll one of the pie crusts to a circle about 11 to 12 inches in diameter. Line the bottom of a 9-inch springform pan with the pie crust so that it comes about 1 1/2 inches up the side of the pan.

In a large bowl, mix together the ricotta cheese, the prepared wheat berries, and sugar until combined. One at a time, beat in the eggs. Mix in the cinnamon, vanilla, and salt until blended. Stir in the candied citrus peel. Transfer the filling to the pie crust in the spring-form pan.

Cut the remaining pie crust into 1/2-inch wide strips and arrange them in a crisscross pattern on top of the filling, trimming the strips as necessary. Press and seal the strips against the edge of the bottom crust. Brush the top of the cheese cake with the melted butter. Bake for about 1 hour, or until golden brown and puffed up. Transfer the pastera to a wire rack and cool completely. When cold, lightly dust the top with confectioners' sugar.

What Are Wheat Berries?

~❦~

Wheat berries are unprocessed whole wheat grains. They are a deep russet brown and shaped like grains of rice. Most of the wheat berries that are sold are hard wheat (also called red wheat). Store the berries in a glass jar with a screw-top lid in a relatively cool place or in the refrigerator. They must be presoaked and then precooked before being used in a recipe. They will still have a firm texture. Bulgur is made from cracked wheat berries.

Marry-Me Chopped Chicken Livers

Makes 4 servings

This is a favorite recipe of segment producer Joanne Saltzman. As a child she had chopped chicken livers a lot at her grandmother's house. Her grandmother served it warm on Ritz crackers, accompanied by tomato juice with lemon wedges. Joanne now likes to offer the same treat when she entertains. She puts out an attractive arrangement of the spread and crackers and lets her guests help themselves while she gets their drinks and completes any last-minute party preparations.

2 tablespoons rendered chicken fat (see page 120)
1 pound fresh chicken livers
2 medium to large onions, cut into quarters
2 hard-cooked eggs
Seasoned salt, pepper, paprika, and garlic powder, to taste
Chopped fresh parsley or parsley sprigs, for garnish
Ritz crackers, rye bread, and other crackers for serving

In a saucepan, melt the chicken fat over low heat. Add the chicken livers and onions. Cover and cook for 20 to 30 minutes, or until the livers are fully cooked through.

Using a slotted spoon, transfer the livers and onions from the pan to a wooden chopping bowl. Add about 2 tablespoons of liquid from the pan (adjust according to how moist you like the mixture to be) to the bowl. Add the eggs. Using a hand chopper, chop the mixture until it is creamy and well combined. Gradually add the seasonings, mixing well after each addition and tasting as you season.

Refrigerate the chopped liver until ready to serve. Let stand at room temperature for about 20 minutes before serving. Arrange it in a mound in the center of the platter, garnish with the parsley, and surround with Ritz crackers, rye bread, and other crackers.

Passover
Orange Roast Brisket

Makes 8 to 10 servings

 Almost every Passover, Rhoda Gelman makes this brisket. Her son, Michael, also makes it when he entertains for Passover. This mother/son duo enjoy cooking so much that they have taken Japanese and Chinese cooking courses together.

Vegetable oil
Salt, pepper, finely chopped garlic, and paprika to taste
5- to 6-pound beef brisket
2 to 3 onions, sliced
2 cups orange juice
1 cup Passover fruit wine
1/4 cup tomato ketchup
1 tablespoon granulated sugar

In a small bowl, stir together the vegetable oil, salt, pepper, garlic, and paprika to form a paste. Rub the meat all over with the mixture. Cover the brisket and let it stand overnight in the refrigerator.

Preheat the oven to 325°F. Arrange half of the sliced onions in the bottom of a roasting pan. Place the meat on top of the onions with the fat side up. In a medium bowl, stir together the orange juice, wine, ketchup, and sugar and pour the mixture over the brisket.

Bake for 3 to 4 hours, or until tender. Let the meat stand for about 30 minutes before carving. Slice the meat against the grain.

Freddie Roman's Mother-in-Law's Potato Pancakes

Makes about 24 pancakes

Actor Freddie Roman was starring in a Broadway play, *Catskills on Broadway*, when he made a guest appearance on "Live." Potato pancakes are a classic Jewish recipe, and Freddie's mother-in-law's version calls for matzoh meal, making it an excellent selection for serving during Passover. Try Freddie's recipe at any time of the year, too; the pancakes are a nice change of pace as a side dish.

6 medium potatoes, peeled
1 large onion, chopped
2 large eggs, lightly beaten
7 tablespoons matzoh meal (or all-purpose flour)
1 teaspoon salt
1/4 teaspoon baking powder
Pinch of ground pepper
2 1/2 tablespoons olive oil

Grate the potatoes in a food processor or by using a handheld grater.

In a large bowl, stir together the potatoes, onion, eggs, matzoh meal, salt, baking powder, and pepper. Let the mixture stand for 5 minutes.

In a large skillet, heat the oil over medium-high heat until the oil is hot enough to brown the potato pancake mixture. Drop the pancake mixture by tablespoonfuls into the oil. Cook the pancakes for 2 to 4 minutes on each side, or until golden brown, turning the pancakes only once. Serve immediately, or place the pancakes in a warm oven until ready to use.

Passover Potato Pudding

Makes 4 to 8 servings

J oan Nathan, author of *Jewish Cooking in America* and *The Jewish Holiday Kitchen*, prepared this soul-satisfying recipe for a special Passover meal. It works equally well as a potato side dish or the main event.

1/4 cup rendered chicken fat (see page 120) or vegetable oil
1 cup chopped onions
1 cup chopped leeks
2 pounds baking potatoes, peeled
4 large eggs, well beaten
2 tablespoons chopped fresh parsley, dill, or basil
Salt and pepper to taste

P reheat the oven to 350°F.

I n a large skillet, heat 2 tablespoons of the chicken fat over medium-high heat. Add the onions and leeks and cook for 7 to 10 minutes, or until golden. Remove from heat.

G rate the potatoes into a large bowl. Stir in the cooled onion mixture, eggs, parsley, salt, and pepper.

H eat the remaining 2 tablespoons of chicken fat and pour the fat into a casserole dish that is large enough to hold the potato mixture. Fold the potato mixture into the chicken fat and smooth the top surface of the pudding.

B ake uncovered for about 50 minutes, or until set and lightly golden on top.

Rendering Chicken Fat

Makes about 2 cups of chicken fat plus *grieben*

Chicken fat and the resulting small squares of crisp chicken skin *(grieben)* are integral to much of Jewish cooking. The technique that follows can also be used for clarifying duck and goose fat. Use a sharp knife to remove the layers of yellow fat and the skin from the fowl.

1 pound unrendered chicken fat and chicken skin
1 small onion, diced

Cut the chicken fat and skin into 1 1/2-inch squares. In a saucepan, over low heat, heat the fat and skin for 5 minutes. Add the diced onion, and continue cooking over low heat until the onion and the bits of skin are lightly browned. Strain the mixture into a jar. The fat will keep almost indefinitely in the jar in the refrigerator.

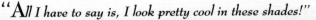

"All I have to say is, I look pretty cool in these shades!"

After the chicken fat has been rendered, reserve the browned *grieben*. Reheat them until they are crisp and hot and serve them as a cocktail tidbit or as a spread with slices of rye bread.

Passover Apple Pudding

Makes 6 servings

Rhoda Gelman makes as much of this satisfying pudding as the number of her guests dictates. She has been known to double, triple, or quadruple this recipe.

3 apples, cored, grated with their skins
3 matzohs, broken up and moistened slightly with water
1 cup raisins
3/4 cup chopped walnuts
1/2 cup granulated sugar
1/2 cup vegetable oil
2 large eggs, lightly beaten
1 1/2 tablespoons freshly squeezed lemon juice
Grated peel of 1/2 lemon or about 1 1/2 tablespoons of
   grated peel
Ground cinnamon to taste

Preheat the oven to 350°F. Oil or butter a 9-inch-square baking pan.

In a large bowl, stir together all the ingredients until combined. Scrape the mixture into the prepared pan and bake for 30 to 60 minutes or until lightly browned on top.

Rhoda's Chocolate Jelly Roll

Makes 12 servings

Even if you run out of room in the refrigerator, Rhoda Gelman advises that you think twice about using the great outdoors as an extra refrigerator. One year, while her guests were inside enjoying dinner, a raccoon dined on one of her exquisite cakes. Serve the following recipe to humans for rave reviews.

    6 ounces semisweet chocolate
    3 tablespoons strong coffee
    5 large eggs, separated
    2/3 cup granulated sugar
    Confectioners' sugar
    1 1/4 cups heavy (whipping) cream
    Unsweetened cocoa powder for dusting the cake

Preheat the oven to 350°F. Lightly butter a large (18-by-21-inch) baking sheet. Line it with waxed paper and butter the waxed paper, as well.

Heat the chocolate and coffee in the top of a double boiler, over hot, not simmering, water until the chocolate is melted, stirring occasionally. Or place the chocolate and the coffee in a microwavable container and microwave at Medium (50 percent power) for 1 to 4 minutes, until the chocolate becomes shiny. Remove the container from the microwave and stir until the chocolate is completely melted. Let the chocolate stand for about 10 minutes, or until tepid.

In a large grease-free bowl, using a rotary beater or a handheld electric mixer set at medium-high speed, beat the egg yolks with the sugar until the mixture is thick and pale in color. Stir in the chocolate mixture.

In another grease-free bowl, using a handheld electric mixer set at medium-high speed, beat the egg whites until stiff peaks just start to form when the beaters are lifted. Using a rubber spatula, fold one-third of the beaten egg whites into the batter to lighten it. Fold in the remaining egg whites.

Spread the mixture evenly over the prepared sheet, leaving about a 1-inch border all around. Bake for 15 minutes, or until a knife inserted in the middle comes out clean. Lightly sprinkle the top of a clean dish towel with confectioners' sugar. Carefully invert the cake onto the towel and immediately peel off the waxed paper. Starting from the short side, roll the cake and towel up together and place the rolled cake and towel on a wire rack to cool completely.

When the cake is completely cool, in a chilled bowl, using a handheld electric mixer fitted with chilled beaters, beat the cream just until stiff enough to spread. Unroll the cake and remove the towel. Spread the cake with some of the whipped cream. Reroll the cake. Place the cake, seam side down, on a serving platter and frost the outside with the remaining whipped cream. Sift cocoa powder lightly over the cake. Refrigerate any leftovers.

Easter Memories
~ ҉ ~

Kathie Lee: We used to color eggs before Easter. I always tried to be very creative with them. My brother dropped every egg into every color, so all his eggs came out gray and exactly the same. I spent years trying to explain to him that you shouldn't do it that way, but that was the way he liked to do it. Probably to this day his kids have gray eggs.

Chapter 7

Mother's Day and Father's Day Favorites

································ ~❦~ ································

Mother's and Father's Days are important occasions for family get-togethers—times to honor the important people who helped to make us what we are today. This chapter is filled with very special dishes that you can design your party around. Mamma Mia Meat Sauce is a standard recipe at all of Kathie Lee's family get-togethers and its name tells us that Joan Epstein, Kathie Lee's mom, is the source of this classic. There is also a recipe from Father Joseph Orsini, cookbook author and priest, for a hearty Italian rice dish. The Clever Cleaver Brothers offer their delicious Clever Shrimp Diego, and "Live" regular Chef Tell has supplied a couple of pork recipes to honor the occasion. Whichever recipes you choose for entertaining, be sure to treat your parents like kings and queens for the day.

$\mathcal{B}$ronzed $\mathcal{C}$hicken $\mathcal{B}$reasts

Makes 4 generous servings

Serve a salad and pasta with this easy three-ingredient recipe for boneless chicken breasts from Chef Paul Prudhomme of K-Paul's Louisiana Kitchen in New Orleans. The secret for getting a "bronzed" finish on the chicken is to make sure your griddle or skillet is hot enough. Chef Paul's recipe gives explicit directions for achieving this in your own kitchen.

> 1/2 cup (1 stick) unsalted (sweet) butter or margarine
> 8 boneless, skinless, chicken breast halves (about 3 ounces each), about 3/4 inch thick at thickest part, at room temperature
> 1 tablespoon plus 1 teaspoon Chef Paul Prudhomme's Poultry Magic (or any of his Magic Seasoning Blends)

Heat a heavy griddle or large, heavy aluminum skillet to 350°F.—about 7 minutes over medium heat (1/2-inch-high flame on a gas stove), or about 23 minutes over medium to medium-low heat on an electric stove. Or use an electric skillet.

$\mathcal{C}$elebrating $\mathcal{M}$other's and $\mathcal{F}$ather's $\mathcal{D}$ays

~ⓔ~

Kathie Lee: For Mother's and Father's Days I try to plant a tree or bush in their memory in the yard—it's something that will last and grow. On Mother's Day, Cody and Frank go shopping, so I usually get some pretty good presents. Now that Cody is in school, he makes me something at school that ends up on the front of the refrigerator.

"What are you trying to do . . . kill me?!" Regis says to Ethel
Senese, his mother-in-law.

Melt the butter in a pie or cake pan. When the griddle or skillet is heated, coat one chicken breast half with warm melted butter. With the chicken in your hand, sprinkle it evenly with about 1/2 teaspoon of Poultry Magic; lay the chicken on the hot griddle or skillet surface. (Don't lay the chicken down on any work surface because the butter and seasoning will adhere to your work surface instead of the chicken.) Continue this procedure for the remaining chicken breasts. Set aside the remaining melted butter in a warm place.

Cook the chicken for 2 to 3 minutes, or until the underside is bronze in color. (Watch and you'll see a white line coming up the sides as the chicken cooks; when the line is about one-half the thickness, the chicken is ready to be turned.) Turn the chicken and drizzle about 1/2 tablespoon of melted butter down the length of each breast. Cook for 2 to 3 minutes more, or until done. Serve immediately, allowing 2 breast halves per person. *Do not overcook!* The chicken should be very juicy.

Chef Tell's Coq au Vin
(Chicken in Wine)

This easy yet elegant dish is from European-trained Chef Tell Erhardt. It's a wonderful dish for entertaining because once it's in the oven, you're free to join your guests. Serve it with rice, a crisp tossed green salad, and chilled white wine.

2 (2 1/2 to 3 pounds each) broiler-frying chickens, cut into
   pieces
Salt and pepper to taste
1/2 cup (1 stick) unsalted (sweet) butter
20 mushroom caps
4 carrots, chopped
2 onions, chopped
1/4 cup all-purpose flour
2 cups dry white wine
2 cups chicken broth

Preheat the oven to 450°F.

Season the chicken with salt and pepper.

In a Dutch oven or a large, heavy ovenproof saucepot, heat the butter over medium-high heat. Add the chicken pieces and cook until lightly browned on all sides.

Stir in the mushrooms, carrots, and onions. Sprinkle the flour over the mixture and stir to coat evenly. Slowly add the wine and chicken broth and stir. Cover the pot and bake for 45 minutes, or until cooked through.

Clever Shrimp Diego

Makes 2 servings

T he Clever Cleaver Brothers, Lee Gerovitz and Steve Cassarino, appeared on "Live" in May with this special dish for mothers. The San Diego–based pair usually dress up in outlandish costumes, but for this segment they came out on the stage in regular chefs' gear. Regis immediately demanded to know what the deal was. The two broke into a Mother's Day rap, meanwhile breaking away their chefs' outfits, which were held together with Velcro, and completed the segment in shorts and tank tops.

Here's their rap:

We're The Clever Cleavers with your Mother's Day surprise.
We'll put a smile on her face, we'll put a twinkle in her eye,
Ta-ta-ta twinkle, ta-ta-ta-twinkle.

Now moms are special, we know they are the best,
They don't come any better, in the East or in the West.

This dish we're gonna make is especially for you,
It's easy to prepare and it's elegant, too.

So make your Mother's Day special, this meal you will enjoy,
A Diego Shrimp from The Clever Cleaver boys!

Serve this recipe over your favorite type of rice or as a filling for heated flour tortillas. Garnish with chopped tomato, sour cream, and sliced olives.

16 large shrimp
1 tablespoon butter
1 tablespoon olive oil
2 garlic cloves, finely chopped
1/4 cup cognac
1/2 cup green chili salsa sauce
2 tablespoons chopped fresh coriander leaves

(continued)

Few dashes of Angostura aromatic bitters
Black pepper to taste

Peel and devein the shrimp. To devein the shrimp, using the point of a sharp knife, make a shallow cut down the center back (the curved side) of each shrimp and remove the dark vein. Rinse away any bits of the vein that remain. Butterfly each shrimp by deepening the cuts made for deveining, cutting almost but not quite through to the underside. Open each shrimp, like a book.

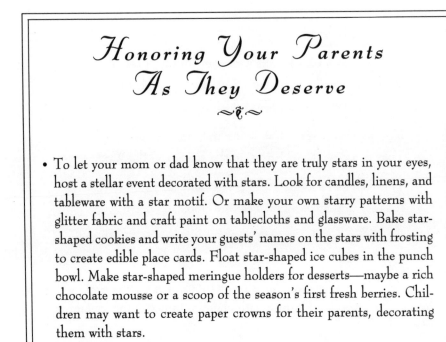

Honoring Your Parents As They Deserve

~❦~

- To let your mom or dad know that they are truly stars in your eyes, host a stellar event decorated with stars. Look for candles, linens, and tableware with a star motif. Or make your own starry patterns with glitter fabric and craft paint on tablecloths and glassware. Bake star-shaped cookies and write your guests' names on the stars with frosting to create edible place cards. Float star-shaped ice cubes in the punch bowl. Make star-shaped meringue holders for desserts—maybe a rich chocolate mousse or a scoop of the season's first fresh berries. Children may want to create paper crowns for their parents, decorating them with stars.

- Offer whipped cream and/or chocolate curls when you serve coffee.

- Create a corsage that won't wilt! Place a photograph of flowers inside a glass slide mount (available from a photo supply catalog or a professional camera store). Glue a jewelry pin on the back.

In a large skillet, heat the butter and oil over medium heat. Cook the garlic for about 30 seconds, stirring frequently. Add the shrimp and cook for about 1 minute on each side. (Do not overcook because the shrimp will continue to cook in the sauce.)

Remove the pan from the heat. Add the cognac. Flame the mixture by touching the cognac with a lighted match. When the flame has died down, stir in the salsa, coriander leaves, and bitters. Season with pepper.

- Go Gatsby with a summer-white decorating scheme—all-white linens, china, and flowers.

- Try a tea-party theme for Mother's Day. Use ceramic and china teapots filled with flowers to decorate the table. Place an individual loaf of fruit bread at each plate. Serve chilled soup in china cups as a first course.

- Set a table that a handy dad will really appreciate. A new red vise surrounded by an abundance of fresh bread becomes a centerpiece. Metal fasteners for rubber plumbing hoses make adjustable napkin rings. Serve ice cream in small empty paint cans—paint stores carry shiny new silver ones—lined with plastic cups. Or you could fill the cans with dad's favorite cookies or candies.

- An omelet bar for mom or a super-long submarine sandwich for dad can be an easy way to celebrate their days. Serve dad's sandwiches on small breadboards instead of plates.

- Use photos of mom or dad enlarged on a photocopier as part of your decor. Use smaller photos on menus or place cards.

- Use a Polaroid camera to record the party and present mom or dad with a mini photo album to take away from a happy day.

Schweinepfeffer
(Peppered Pork)

Makes 2 to 4 servings

Chef Tell Erhardt won the Culinary Olympics in 1970 in Stuttgart, Germany, with this delicious recipe for pork. He has won the award several times. Tell is not only a skilled chef; he also manufactures and sells his own products under the Health Craft logo. They include stainless steel cookware, American-made knives, and his exclusive 24-karat gold-handled Chef Tell collection cookware.

> 2 tablespoons vegetable oil
> 12 ounces pork loin, cut into thin slices
> 1 cup thinly sliced mushrooms
> 1 cup chopped onions
> Cracked black pepper to taste
> Salt to taste
> 1/2 cup red wine
> 1/2 cup chopped parsley
> Freshly cooked noodles or spätzle

Heat a large skillet over high heat until very hot. Carefully add the oil and then the pork strips.

Add the mushrooms, onions, pepper, and salt. Continue cooking for 2 to 3 minutes, or until cooked through, stirring frequently.

Using a slotted spoon, remove the pork from the skillet and keep warm. Add the wine to the skillet and continue cooking until the mixture is reduced by half. Stir in the parsley, then return the meat to the skillet. Serve with freshly cooked noodles or spätzle.

Pork Loin Madrid

Makes 4 servings

 Chef Tell also demonstrated another pork dish, this time a Spanish-style creation. Make sure to remove only the green part of the lime when you grate the peel. The white part tends to be bitter.

1 fresh lime
4 slices (4 ounces each) boneless pork loin
1/2 cup olive oil, divided
2 garlic cloves, finely chopped
Cracked black pepper to taste
Fresh or dried thyme leaves to taste
Fresh or dried basil leaves to taste
All-purpose flour for dredging the pork
1/2 cup white wine

Grate the peel from the lime and reserve. Juice the lime and reserve.

In a bowl, combine the pork with 5 tablespoons of the olive oil, garlic, the reserved grated lime peel, pepper, thyme, and basil. Cover and refrigerate for at least 1 hour or overnight.

Remove the pork from the marinade and dip each slice in turn in flour to lightly coat both sides; shake off any excess.

In a large skillet, heat the remaining 3 tablespoons of oil over medium-high heat. Cook the pork slices for 7 to 10 minutes on each side, or until cooked through. Add the wine and reserved lime juice and heat through.

Grilled Fish

Francis Anthony, the Love Chef, appeared on "Live" just before Father's Day to demonstrate this terrific recipe. Bake potatoes and serve a nice tossed salad as accompaniments to the fish.

3/4 cup dry white wine
1/2 cup olive oil
3 tablespoons dry bread crumbs
2 tablespoons freshly squeezed lime juice
1/2 teaspoon dried basil leaves
Dash of hot pepper sauce
Ground black pepper and salt to taste
1 whole fish (2 to 5 pounds) of your choice, cleaned

In a shallow glass dish, combine all the ingredients except the fish. Add the fish to the marinade, cover, and refrigerate for 30 minutes, basting frequently with the marinade.

Using a paper towel, lightly rub a little vegetable oil on the grill or broiler pan. Position the grill or broiler 5 to 6 inches away from the heat source. Cook the fish for 10 to 20 minutes on each side (depending on its thickness), or until the fish is cooked through, basting frequently with the marinade.

Rice Calabrese Style

Makes 4 servings

This recipe from Father Joseph Orsini seems particularly appropriate for this chapter. Father Orsini has produced his own cookbook, *Father Orsini's Italian Kitchen.* He selected this recipe to demonstrate on "Live" because it is easy to make and tastes marvelous. "Calabrese" means that this recipe is prepared using the style of cooking from Calabria, the southernmost region of Italy on the toe of the peninsula. This is where Father Orsini's parents are from. Father Orsini likes to accompany his rice and potato dish with a fresh green salad tossed with an oil and vinegar dressing, and with crispy Italian bread.

2 tablespoons olive oil
1 large onion, finely sliced
1 small garlic clove, finely chopped
1 teaspoon salt
1 teaspoon crushed red pepper flakes
2 cans (8 ounces each) tomato sauce
2 potatoes, peeled and diced
4 cups cooked rice
Grated Parmesan cheese for sprinkling on top

In a large saucepan, heat the oil over low heat. Cook the onion, garlic, salt, and pepper for about 10 minutes, or until the onion is softened but not browned. Stir in the tomato sauce and potatoes and simmer over low heat, stirring occasionally, for 1 hour. Stir in the cooked rice and serve hot. Sprinkle with Parmesan cheese at the table.

Mamma Mia Meat Sauce

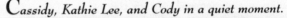

Makes 10 servings

athie Lee's sister, Michie Mader, recently paid a culinary visit to her sister's show with a great dish for parties. This recipe makes a jumbo amount of meat sauce, and its inviting aroma as it cooks primes everyone for the upcoming meal. Michie reports that at family get-togethers, she and Frank do all the cooking. The day that Michie was cooking on the show, she was wearing a fabulous white outfit—much too nice to cover up with an apron but also not the ideal attire for cooking tomato sauce; Regis pretended to be mystified as to why Michie kept her distance from the bubbling sauce.

Michie says it's easy to create a complete meal by smothering some pasta with this sauce and offering it with garlic bread, a green

Cassidy, Kathie Lee, and Cody in a quiet moment.

salad, and red wine. For smaller groups, make the whole amount and freeze leftovers for use at another time.

 2 pounds ground chuck (or ground turkey)
 4 cans (28 ounces each) tomato sauce
 1 can (16 ounces) tomato paste
 1 large onion, diced
 3/4 to 1 cup dried parsley leaves
 2 tablespoons olive oil
 2 teaspoons crushed garlic
 1/2 teaspoon dried oregano leaves
 Salt and pepper to taste
 Spaghetti, cooked according to package directions

In a large saucepot, cook the beef over medium heat until it is well browned. Drain off the fat and discard.

Add the tomato sauce, tomato paste, onion, parsley, oil, garlic, oregano, salt, and pepper. Bring the mixture to a boil and then simmer, uncovered, for 1 1/2 hours, stirring frequently. Serve over cooked spaghetti.

Chapter 8

The Race Is On– Kentucky Derby Day

·············· ~❦~ ··············

Probably the most famous horse race in the United States is the Kentucky Derby. Whether you are lucky enough to be at Churchill Downs or are simply having a party in honor of this rite of spring, you'll want to celebrate in style. Robin Leach, a frequent pinch-hitter co-host for "Live," knows how to serve up "champagne wishes and caviar dreams," and he has contributed several recipes to this chapter. Start your party with his layered Caviar Pie. For the main course, serve his Rich and Famous Chicken accompanied by Riz Pilaf. For dessert, splash champagne over fresh fruit and serve it while it is still bubbly.

For the Love Chef's Kentucky Derby appearance on "Live,"

he prepared his saucy recipe for Bourbon Chicken, which is sure to be a winner for you, too. If you are headed for a party, make sure to bring along a pan of Joanna Philbin's extra-chocolaty brownies for your favorite chocolate lovers.

Tips for Your Derby Day Get-Together

~ℓ~

- A few weeks ahead of time, start collecting data on the race and on the horses that are running. Assemble the material in a notebook, or mount it on posters around the room so that your guests can make educated "bets."

- Mint juleps are an obvious choice, but not the only beverage to serve. Think of Planter's Punch, Ramos Gin Fizzes, and Southern Comfort. To comfort the soft drinkers, offer a really well-made iced tea.

- Play blue-grass music in the background.

- Large trays with small amounts of canapés or cold cuts look dramatic.

- Just-washed cherry tomatoes make a bright hors d'oeuvre when paired with a dish of sea salt mixed with a couple of teaspoons of Italian seasoning. Guests dip the tomatoes into the salt, then pop them into their mouths. For a Tex-Mex version, add a small saucer of tequila for dipping the tomatoes into before the salt.

- Use horseshoes as part of your decorations.

Robin Leach's Caviar Pie

Robin Leach, executive producer and host of "Lifestyles of the Rich and Famous" and "Run Away with the Rich and Famous," has been wined and dined in some of the world's most fabulous locations by some of the world's most extraordinary people. In fact, Robin has published his own cookbook, *The Lifestyles of the Rich and Famous Cookbook*. This recipe is an easy and inspired appetizer that you will make again and again. Use as much caviar as you can afford.

1 to 4 ounces of caviar
8 ounces cream cheese, softened
1/4 cup mayonnaise
2 to 3 teaspoons grated onion
1 to 2 teaspoons Worcestershire sauce
1 to 2 teaspoons freshly squeezed lemon juice
Chopped fresh parsley
1 hard-cooked egg, peeled and grated
Finely chopped red onion
Melba toast rounds

Rinse and drain the caviar. Set aside on paper towels to drain thoroughly.

In a medium bowl, stir together the cream cheese and mayonnaise until well blended. Season the mixture with the grated onion, Worcestershire sauce, and lemon juice.

Spread the mixture in the center of a plate or a tray so that it forms a circle about 1 inch thick. Cover the top with the caviar and then sprinkle the parsley all around the outside edge. Sprinkle the grated egg and the onion over the top. Chill and serve with melba toast rounds.

Essence of Silver and Gold

Makes about 4 cups

Robin knows that a flavorful stock is the basis of many an outstanding recipe. Here is his recipe for an extraordinary stock that uses wine. Robin advises, "Use your best wine for this sauce. Spare not and the results will pay off in praise." Of course, "Mr. Champagne" likes to use champagne. This stock recipe makes 4 cups—enough for preparing the two recipes that follow.

2 (1-pound) pieces of bottom round of veal, boned and tied
2 whole chicken breasts, about 1 pound each, bone in
2 whole cloves
2 large onions
4 pounds veal bones, cut into 3 or 4 large pieces
2 leeks, trimmed, washed thoroughly, and coarsely chopped
2 celery stalks, thickly sliced
2 medium carrots, halved and thickly sliced
3 to 4 branches fresh thyme or 2 teaspoons dried thyme
    leaves
20 whole black peppercorns
2 bay leaves
2 teaspoons salt
12 cups water
4 cups good-quality dry white wine

Trim the veal and chicken of any visible fat. Insert a clove in each onion.

Combine all the ingredients in a large, nonreactive stockpot, adding the water and wine last. Bring the mixture to a boil over high heat, then reduce the heat to low and simmer, uncovered, for 2 to 3 hours, or until the liquid measures about 4 cups. Periodically skim off any residue that rises to the top.

Line a large sieve or colander with a double layer of cheesecloth or coarse muslin and set it inside a large bowl. Carefully ladle in the hot stock, discarding the solids. Cover and refrigerate. Remove any fat that hardens on top. Store in the freezer for later use.

Getting ready for a big season, Regis warms up on the set.

Robin Leach's "Rich-and-Famous Chicken"

Makes 4 to 6 servings

 When Robin is not out reporting on the rich and famous, he does most of his entertaining on Friday and Saturday nights at his retreat on a lake in Connecticut. He keeps his freezer filled with stocks and sauces for pasta, and says that "the champagne is always chilling in the fridge." Robin is an avid collector of pottery plates, especially those with colorful Caribbean themes, and he likes to serve this recipe on one of the plates.

8 tablespoons (1 stick) unsalted (sweet) butter, divided
3 tablespoons all-purpose flour
2 cups Essence of Silver and Gold (recipe precedes)
Salt and freshly ground pepper to taste
2 large onions (about 1 pound), sliced
1 whole chicken (3 1/2 to 5 pounds), cut into 8 pieces
1 cup champagne, divided
1/4 cup finely chopped fresh basil leaves or 2 tablespoons
   dried basil leaves
2 tablespoons finely chopped fresh oregano leaves or 1
   tablespoon dried oregano leaves
1 tablespoon freshly squeezed lemon juice
2 teaspoons steak sauce
1/2 teaspoon dry mustard
1/2 pound white mushrooms, trimmed, wiped clean, and
   thinly sliced
1 pound carrots, trimmed, peeled, halved, and cut into
   1-inch-thick slices
1 cup green peas
4 medium potatoes (about 2 pounds), peeled and cut into
   1/2-inch cubes
1 cup heavy (whipping) cream

"For this I come to work every day?"

While Regis polishes up his surfboard, Kathie Lee checks out the waves.

"Watch it, Reege. You're next!"

Kathie Lee and Frank joke around during a show.

*Christina Ferrare and MTV's Duff enjoy watching Regis
do his best Conehead impression.*

Regis and his co-host, the San Diego Chicken, sing out with everything they've got — heart, soul, and feathers!

Kathie Lee enjoys a hug with Frank as Regis pokes fun.

Regis and Kathie Lee watch Linda Blair's reaction
to the Devilish Split Pea Soup.

Regis and Kathie Lee feed each other bites of
Joanie's Sweet and Sour Chicken.

*Regis samples pasta while Kathie Lee "negotiates"
her contract with executive producer Michael Gelman.*

*Kathie Lee's mom and dad, Joan and Aaron Epstein,
look on as Kathie Lee tries to convince Regis to "Open wide!"*

"You look soooo cute!"

Joy, daughter Joanna, Michael Gelman, Regis, and segment producer Barbara Fight pose after the wedding fashion show.

Joy and Regis marvel at baby Cassidy,
while Kathie Lee gives Cody a squeeze.

The Philbin family celebrates Christmas. From left to right:
Joanna, Joy, Regis, and Jennifer.

Preheat the oven to 425°F. for a baking dish or 475°F. for a clay pot.

In a medium heavy saucepan, melt 3 tablespoons of the butter over medium-high heat. Stir in the flour. Reduce the heat to medium and cook slowly for 3 to 5 minutes, whisking constantly, until well blended. Stir in the Essence of Silver and Gold and bring the mixture to a boil. Reduce the heat and simmer for 7 to 10 minutes, or until the sauce is thickened and smooth, stirring often. Season with salt and pepper. Remove the pan from the heat and keep warm.

Place the sliced onions in the bottom of an ovenproof clay pot or baking dish. Cut 2 1/2 tablespoons of the butter into thin slices and distribute them evenly over the onions.

Rinse the chicken pieces with water and pat dry with paper towels. Season with salt and pepper. Place the chicken on top of the onions and sprinkle with 2 tablespoons of the champagne. Add the basil, oregano, lemon juice, steak sauce, and mustard.

Arrange the mushrooms, carrots, and peas on top of the chicken. Top with thin slices of the remaining butter. Sprinkle with 2 more tablespoons of the champagne.

Pour the Essence of Silver and Gold over the chicken and sprinkle with the remaining champagne. Sink the potato cubes into the sauce, leaving them only slightly submerged. Cover the pot tightly and bake for about 45 to 50 minutes, or until the vegetables are soft and the chicken is cooked through.

Remove the cover and cook about 10 minutes longer, or until the protruding bits of potato are lightly browned.

Arrange the chicken and vegetables on a serving platter. Cover to keep warm. In a medium saucepan over high heat, boil the cream for 3 to 5 minutes, or until reduced by half. Add the reduced cream to the pan juices and boil for several minutes to reduce and thicken slightly. Pour the mixture over the chicken and serve immediately.

$\mathcal{R}iz$ $\mathcal{P}ilaf$

Makes 4 servings

 Here's the very special rice side dish that Robin makes using Essence of Silver and Gold.

1 cup long-grain white rice
2 tablespoons (1/4 stick) unsalted (sweet) butter
1 large onion, coarsely chopped
1/2 teaspoon salt
1/4 teaspoon freshly ground pepper
1/8 teaspoon ground cumin
2 cups Essence of Silver and Gold (page 142)
Additional salt and pepper to taste

Preheat the oven to 325°F. Rinse the rice under cold water. In a medium, flame-proof casserole with a tight-fitting lid, melt the butter over medium-high heat. Add the onion and cook for about 3 minutes, or until it is softened but not browned. Stir in the salt, pepper, and cumin. Stir in the rice. Reduce the heat to medium and stir for 2 to 3 minutes, or until the rice is coated and slightly transparent.

Meanwhile, bring the Essence of Silver and Gold to a boil. Pour it over the rice mixture and stir well. Cover the casserole and bake for 20 minutes. Remove from the oven. Stir gently to separate the grains of rice and replace the lid. Let stand 5 minutes longer. Season with additional salt and pepper, if necessary. Serve at once.

Bourbon Chicken

 For the Love Chef's Kentucky Derby visit to "Live," he demonstrated, most appropriately, the following recipe for bourbon chicken.

2 tablespoons (1/4 stick) unsalted (sweet) butter
2 whole chicken breasts, cut in half
1/2 cup bourbon, divided
4 to 6 shallots, sliced
1/2 cup heavy (whipping) cream
1/4 teaspoon ground white pepper
1/8 teaspoon ground nutmeg

In a large skillet, heat the butter over medium heat. Add the chicken breasts, skin side down. Pour 1/4 cup of the bourbon over the chicken. Flame the chicken by touching the bourbon with a lighted match and let the flame burn down.

Add the shallots and the remaining 1/4 cup of bourbon. Reduce the heat to medium-low, cover the skillet and cook for 45 to 55 minutes, or until the chicken is cooked through. Transfer the chicken to a warm serving platter.

Drain off and discard any excess fat. Using a wooden spoon, scrape the pan to loosen the browned bits from the bottom of the skillet. Stir in the cream, pepper, and nutmeg and simmer until the sauce is thickened, stirring frequently. Pour the sauce over the chicken and serve.

Catherine Scorsese's
Lemon and Garlic Chicken

When actress Catherine Scorsese appeared on "Live," she prepared a recipe for a flavorful low-fat dish with chicken. Catherine, mother of the film director Martin Scorsese, is currently hard at work on a cookbook of family recipes that is due out in 1995.

As she added the substantial amount of garlic this recipe calls for, Catherine said to Regis, "For sure you will sleep alone if you eat this dish." (In fact, Joy frequently leaves their bedroom when, she says, Regis's snoring gets to be too much.) Catherine admits that the quantities for the recipe ingredients are approximate. She amused Regis and the viewers with her quip: "The old folks didn't measure. Hey, if it came out good, it came out good. If it didn't, too bad."

After she finished making the recipe, actor Joe Pesci, a close family friend (Catherine calls him her number-three son), delighted her with a surprise visit to sample her specialty. Everyone gave the dish rave reviews. To complete the meal, Catherine likes to serve roasted potatoes, a salad of roasted red peppers with olive oil and vinegar, and ripe olives.

> 2 1/2 pounds of chicken parts
> 8 large or 12 small lemons
> 1/4 cup chopped fresh parsley
> 2 teaspoons olive oil
> Large whole head of garlic
> Salt and pepper to taste

Remove the skin from the chicken pieces (and as much as possible from the wings). Rinse the chicken and pat dry with paper towels.

Roll the lemons on a hard surface in order to soften them. Squeeze the lemons and put the juice in a bowl. Stir in the parsley and olive oil.

Peel the garlic cloves and cut each clove into lengthwise slivers. Add them to the lemon juice.

Place the chicken in a baking dish. Pour half of the lemon juice mixture over the chicken and let stand for about 15 minutes.

Preheat the oven to 350°F. Bake the chicken for about 30 minutes, then turn the pieces over and cook for another 20 minutes. If desired, you can remove the pieces of chicken from the juice and place them under the broiler for a couple of minutes to brown. Serve the remaining lemon juice mixture with the chicken. Season to taste.

Regis cheers for his alma mater: "Go, Notre Dame!"

Linguine with White Clam Sauce

Makes 2 to 4 servings

Singing chef Nicola Paone, of Paone's restaurant in Manhattan, demonstrated this easy recipe. To make it even easier, substitute canned clams for the fresh clams.

8 cherrystone clams
1/2 pound linguine
4 tablespoons olive oil, divided
1 garlic clove, crushed
8 shrimp, shelled and diced (optional)
2 tablespoons chopped fresh parsley
Salt and pepper to taste

Scrub the clams well to remove any grit. Place the clams in a large saucepan. Add about 1 cup of boiling water. Cover the pan and cook over medium heat for 5 to 7 minutes, or until the shells open. Reserve the cooking liquid. Remove the meat from the shells and chop.

Bring a large pot of salted water to a boil. Add the pasta and cook just until *al dente*. Drain thoroughly and keep warm.

Meanwhile, in another saucepan, heat 3 tablespoons of the olive oil over medium-high heat. Add the garlic clove and cook for 1 to 3 minutes, or until browned. Discard the garlic. Add the chopped clams, 2 to 3 tablespoons of the reserved clam broth, and the shrimp, if you are using them. When the mixture comes to a boil, turn off the heat and add the parsley. Season with salt and pepper. Add the white clam sauce and the remaining 1 tablespoon of olive oil to the cooked linguine and toss to combine.

Cynthia's Pasta Primavera Supreme

In this appealing and versatile recipe from Cynthia Lockhart, production secretary of "Live," the vegetables are roasted before they are tossed with freshly cooked pasta, Parmesan cheese, and herbs. The recipe can be served as a main course, or as a side dish with Italian sausage, spare ribs, or barbecued chicken. The most memorable party Cynthia remembers attending was given by a collector friend who created a theme for every room in his house: One was a hat room, with hats all over it. A chair room had chairs everywhere, even hanging from the ceiling, and the bathroom was decorated with golf clubs.

2 green bell peppers, seeded and cut into 1/2-inch-wide
   strips
2 red bell peppers, seeded and cut into 1/2-inch-wide strips
2 yellow bell peppers, seeded and cut into 1/2-inch-wide
   strips
2 red onions, cut into 1/2-inch-thick slices
1 medium eggplant, cut into 1-inch chunks
1 yellow squash, cut into 1/2-inch-thick slices
4 garlic cloves, finely chopped
1/4 cup extra-virgin olive oil
1 pound ziti, penne, or other type of pasta
3 tablespoons grated Parmesan cheese
1 tablespoon chopped fresh parsley
1 teaspoon dried basil leaves, crumbled
Salt and pepper to taste

Preheat the oven to 400°F. Spread the vegetables in a large roasting pan. Drizzle the olive oil over the vegetables and toss to coat them with the oil. Bake for about 35 minutes, or until the vegetables are tender.

(continued)

Bring a large pot of salted water to a boil. Add the pasta and cook just until *al dente.* Drain thoroughly.

In a large serving bowl, toss the pasta with the vegetables. Add the Parmesan, parsley, basil, salt, and pepper.

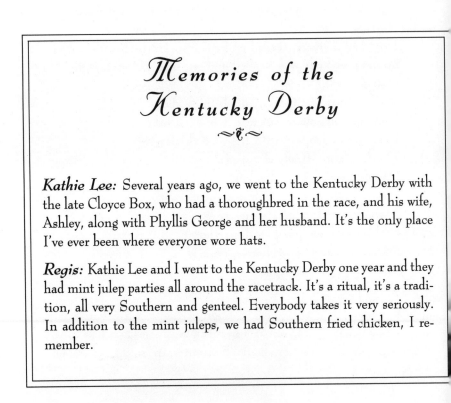

Memories of the
Kentucky Derby

Kathie Lee: Several years ago, we went to the Kentucky Derby with the late Cloyce Box, who had a thoroughbred in the race, and his wife, Ashley, along with Phyllis George and her husband. It's the only place I've ever been where everyone wore hats.

Regis: Kathie Lee and I went to the Kentucky Derby one year and they had mint julep parties all around the racetrack. It's a ritual, it's a tradition, all very Southern and genteel. Everybody takes it very seriously. In addition to the mint juleps, we had Southern fried chicken, I remember.

Joanna's
Exam-cramming Brownies

Makes about 20 brownies

Joanna Philbin, Regis's daughter, appeared on "Live" and demonstrated her indulgent recipe for brownies. Pure unsweetened chocolate gives these brownies a rich chocolate flavor, and they become even more decadent and chocolaty with the addition of chocolate chips. This dessert was one of Joanna's favorites when she was a little girl; now she treats herself and her friends with these brownies when she feels that she needs a reward or a booster—as at exam time. Leave them in the pan for carrying to picnics or parties.

1 cup (2 sticks) unsalted (sweet) butter
4 ounces unsweetened chocolate
2 cups granulated sugar
4 large eggs, at room temperature
1 cup all-purpose flour
1 teaspoon vanilla extract
2 cups miniature marshmallows
1 cup chopped pecans
1 1/2 cups semisweet chocolate chips, divided

Preheat the oven to 350°F. Butter a 13-by-9-inch baking pan.

Melt the butter and chocolate in a dish in the microwave oven or in a saucepan over low heat on the stove. When the mixture is melted, transfer it to a large bowl.

Using a wooden spoon, stir in the sugar until combined. Stir in the eggs until blended. Stir in the flour and vanilla. Stir in the marshmallows, pecans, and 1 cup of the chocolate chips. Scrape the mixture into the prepared pan and spread it evenly. Sprinkle the remaining 1/2 cup of chocolate chips evenly over the top of the brownies.

(continued)

Bake for 40 to 45 minutes, or until cooked through and a toothpick inserted 2 inches from the center comes out with a few moist crumbs clinging to it. Transfer the pan with the brownies to a wire rack and cool for at least 10 minutes before cutting into squares. Cool completely before removing the squares.

Packing Cookies or Bars for Shipping

~❦~

*P*erhaps you know someone who could use a little reward or is just getting ready to cram for an exam! Here are a some pointers on how to pack baked goods so that they arrive intact.

- Whenever you send packages containing food, make sure to mark the container with the words "perishable" and "fragile."

- Label both the inside and outside of the box in case the outer label is torn off.

- For extra freshness, wrap each bar or cookie individually in foil or plastic wrap before packing it in a container. Or wrap cookies in stacks.

- Insulate the top and bottom of the container with crumpled waxed or tissue paper, plain popcorn, plastic bubble wrap, or plastic foam pellets. Use additional packing material to fill all spaces snugly.

- Pack the cookies or bars close together so that they won't be jostled during transit.

- Pack heavier baked goods at the bottom of the container.

- For added durability, pack the box of bars or cookies inside a larger box that you have filled with cushioning material.

- Last, but not least, pack the bars or cookies in an attractive container or tin, and include the recipe as a special treat. Even plain boxes can be jazzed up by being covered with festive gift wrap.

~❦~

Chapter 9

Memorable Memorial Days

·········~ 🍷 ~·········

M emorial Day marks the beginning of the summer and the official start of warm weather get-togethers. It's the time of year when our patios beckon us to come out and use them, when we unpack our picnic gear and turn again to partying outdoors.

This chapter features recipes that tend to be on the lighter side and make use of seafood and chicken. The Love Chef's recipe, Neptune's Fantasy, is an innovative creation calling for several types of seafood and vegetables, seasoned with herbs and white wine. Everything is wrapped together in an aluminum foil package and cooked on the grill. You can assemble the package ahead of time and keep it chilled until you cook it on your backyard grill or tote it to a picnic area for a gourmet twist on a barbecue. Joan Epstein, Kathie Lee's mother, offers her recipe for an extra-easy pasta and seafood salad, as well as a recipe for a special accompaniment salad—both family favorites. For your Memorial Day dessert, serve Fred and Linda Griffith's Blueberry Cobbler to take advantage of the fresh blueberries that are in plentiful supply at this time of year.

Making Your Memorial Day Memorable

~❦~

- Be sure to display your American flag and take time to reflect on what this day is really all about.

- For a portable salad course, place a couple of tablespoons of a creamy dressing in the bottom of red, white, and blue plastic cups, one for each person in the party. Then stand an assortment of carrot and celery sticks and strips of red and green pepper in each cup.

- For a Memorial Day remembrance that will last for more than one day, give guests tree seedlings (available from your local Agricultural Extension office) to plant at home.

- A roll of red- or blue-striped awning fabric makes a great stain-resistant table cover that can be used year after year.

- For tidy picnic transport, pack each guest's meal, utensils, tableware, and glasses individually in a brightly colored shopping bag. And bring along waterproof totes or plastic garbage bags for carrying recyclables home.

- Add zest to holiday hot dogs and hamburgers with an international condiment bar. Sauerkraut and beer mustard for German dogs, blue cheese and watercress for French burgers, jalapeño cheese and salsa for Mexican burgers and dogs, pizza sauce and mozzarella for an Italian flavor, and peanut sauce and bean sprouts for Asian-inspired burgers and dogs.

- A basket or platter of bell peppers—green, red, yellow, orange, and purple—makes an inexpensive and appealing summer centerpiece.

- Transport muffins in their own baking tins so that they don't crumble and break apart.

- Fill an insulated container with chilled gazpacho for an easy soup course. Pass herbed croutons and sour cream as garnishes.

Hunting Hill Farm
Layered Mexican Dip

Makes 6 to 8 servings

 Robin Shallow, a production executive for Buena Vista Television, is a big fan of her mother's layered Mexican dip recipe. While Robin was growing up, her family moved a lot, but the place they most called home was Hunting Hill Farm in Colorado. Mexican food is very popular in Colorado and her mother would serve this dip before a Mexican-style meal that might include green chili soup, enchilada casserole, or chilies relleños. The dip is great with margaritas and beer, and you can adjust the recipe to whatever you have on hand. For a spur-of-the-moment dip, stir together a 16-ounce can of refried beans with a 4-ounce can of chopped green chilies and heat in the microwave.

    1 can (16 ounces) refried beans
    About 1 ounce of Velveeta, broken into pieces
    3 tablespoons milk
    2 ripe avocados, peeled and pitted
    2 teaspoons freshly squeezed lemon juice
    1/4 to 1/2 teaspoon garlic salt
    1 large tomato, chopped
    1 cup sliced ripe olives
    1/3 cup chopped scallions, including the tender green tops
    1/4 cup sliced jalapeño peppers (or to taste)
    1 1/2 cups grated colby or cheddar cheese
    1 container (8 ounces) sour cream

In a microwave-safe bowl, stir together the refried beans, Velveeta, and milk. Microwave on High for 30 to 60 seconds or until heated through and the Velveeta has melted.

Spread the refried bean mixture evenly over the bottom of a 9-inch glass plate. *(continued)*

In a bowl, mash together the avocados, lemon juice, and garlic salt until combined. Spread the avocado mixture over the beans. Sprinkle the tomato, olives, scallions, and jalapeño peppers evenly over the top. Sprinkle the grated cheese over the top and spoon the sour cream in dollops on top of the dip. Serve with tortilla chips and crackers.

"Who's the chef here, me or you?!" Regis asks comedian Freddie Roman.

California Roll

Walt Disney World was the setting for Chef Jiro Tominaga's demonstration on "Live". Jiro is the chef at Mitsukoshi Restaurant in the Japan Pavilion, a favorite restaurant of Regis's. California Roll is a type of sushi that, as Kathie Lee pointed out, does *not* contain raw fish. You will need a small, flexible bamboo mat (they are sold in Asian stores) to help you roll the sushi.

2 cups uncooked long-grain white rice
1/4 cup rice vinegar
1 tablespoon plus 1 teaspoon sugar
1 tablespoon plus 1 teaspoon salt
10 sheets (8-by-7 1/2 inches each) of toasted seaweed (nori)
1/2 cup sesame seeds
8 ounces of crabmeat or imitation crabmeat, shredded
2 tablespoons mayonnaise
1/2 ripe avocado, cut lengthwise into 1/8-inch-diameter strips
1/2 cucumber, cut lengthwise into 1/8-inch-diameter strips
2 ounces smelt roe or any kind of caviar
Soy sauce, for dipping the rolls (optional)

Cook the rice according to the package directions. Stir in the vinegar, sugar, and salt until combined. Cool to room temperature.

Place each sheet of seaweed so that the 8-inch-long side is closest to you. Spread about 3/4 cup of the rice mixture evenly over one half of each sheet of seaweed to form a layer about 3 3/4 by 8 inches and about 1/2 inch thick. Sprinkle a scant 1 tablespoon of the sesame seeds evenly over the surface of the rice on each piece of seaweed.

Have a bamboo mat ready on a flat surface. Place a 12-inch square piece of plastic wrap over the top of each sesame-topped sheet of seaweed. Holding the layers together, flip one of the sheets over onto the mat so that the plastic wrap rests on the mat and the section with the rice faces away from you. *(continued)*

In a medium bowl, stir together the crabmeat and mayonnaise until combined.

Arrange a tenth of the avocado strips so that they run lengthwise down the center of each piece of seaweed. Top with a tenth of the crabmeat mixture and then a tenth of the strips of cucumber. Sprinkle a little of the roe evenly over the top. Fold the bottom edge of the seaweed to the top edge, bringing the mat and plastic wrap to the top as well. Use the mat to roll the seaweed around the filling, squeezing it together firmly as you roll it. As you roll it, keep the plastic wrap loose. Repeat the process for each piece of seaweed. You should end up with a cylinder with the filling running through the center and the rice around the outside.

Remove the plastic wrap from the roll. Cut the roll into rounds that are each about 1 inch wide. Repeat the process to fill each of the remaining sheets of seaweed. Serve with individual portions of soy sauce, for dipping, if desired.

Neptune's Fantasy

On warm summer days, no one wants to spend time indoors over a hot stove. This "meal-in-a-packet" from the Love Chef can be made on the grill. It could also be made in the oven. Fruit salad and a freshly made loaf of bread would be nice accompaniments.

1/4 cup olive oil
8 medium shrimp, peeled and deveined
1/4 pound scallops
8 littleneck clams
6 ounces red snapper fillet
1 carrot, sliced
1/2 head of broccoli, cut into florets
1/2 head of cauliflower, cut into florets
3 large mushrooms, cut into quarters
1 whole bay leaf, crumbled
1/4 teaspoon dried oregano leaves
Pinch of dried marjoram leaves
Pinch of crushed red pepper flakes
Salt and pepper to taste
1/2 cup white wine
Juice of 1/2 lemon

Coat one side of a large piece of heavy-duty extra-wide aluminum with the oil. Place all the seafood in the center of one half of the foil. (The other half will cover the food.)

Leave any excess water clinging to the vegetables and place them on top of the seafood. Turn up the edges of the foil so that the liquid will not escape. Sprinkle the vegetables with the bay leaf, oregano, marjoram, and red pepper flakes. Season with salt and pepper. Add the wine and lemon juice. Bring the other half of the foil down over the food and carefully fold the two edges together all the way around so that you seal the packet. *(continued)*

Place the foil packet on the grill and cook for about 20 to 25 minutes, then check to see if the fish is done by carefully opening one side of the packet. If your grill has a lid, you can open the top of the packet after the first 15 minutes of cooking and finish cooking with the grill lid closed. If you are using a gas or electric grill, set the heat at medium-low. Remove the bay leaf.

F*red and Linda Griffith from "Cleveland Morning Exchange"*
laugh at Regis's jokes while preparing a feast.

Joanie's Pasta à la Treat

Makes 4 to 6 servings

This easy family favorite happened by chance when Kathie Lee's mother, Joan Epstein, was cleaning out the refrigerator! If you are lucky enough to have the ingredients on hand in *your* refrigerator, make a spur-of-the-moment picnic luncheon on the patio or porch. Joan serves her seafood and pasta creation with crescent rolls and the recipe for Carol's California Salad that follows.

6 ounces thin spaghetti
1 pound imitation crabmeat
2 scallions, sliced
3/4 cup low-fat or regular mayonnaise

Bring a large pot of salted water to a boil. Break the spaghetti into thirds and cook it just until *al dente*. Drain.

Break the imitation crabmeat into small pieces. Combine all of the ingredients. It's best to let the salad chill for at least 3 hours before serving to allow the flavors to blend.

Carol's California Salad

 This refreshing salad was given to Joan Epstein by her dear friend Carol Kilgore, of Ottawa, Canada. It can easily be turned into a main dish with the addition of grilled strips of chicken breast.

SALAD
1 medium head romaine lettuce, torn into bite-size pieces
1 can (11 ounces) mandarin oranges, drained
2 tablespoons sliced almonds (toasted if desired)
1 medium carrot, sliced into thin rounds

DRESSING
1/4 cup vegetable oil
2 tablespoons white vinegar
2 tablespoons granulated sugar
Pinch of salt

To Make the Salad: In a large bowl, toss together the lettuce, oranges, almonds, and carrot.

To Make the Dressing: In a small glass measuring cup or small bowl, stir together all of the ingredients.

Pour the dressing ingredients over the salad and toss to coat thoroughly.

Chicken Breasts with Fresh Tomato and Garlic

Makes 2 to 4 servings

 Pierre Franey, master of sophisticated meals in minutes, prepared the following main course for the viewers of "Live." In addition to being the author of the cookbook *Cuisine Rapide,* Pierre is also a columnist for *The New York Times.*

5 medium plum tomatoes
2 tablespoons olive oil
4 boneless, skinless chicken breast halves
4 large garlic cloves, unpeeled
1/2 cup finely chopped onions
1/2 cup dry white wine
1 bay leaf
1/2 teaspoon dried thyme leaves
Salt and pepper to taste

Submerge the tomatoes in boiling water for about 30 seconds to loosen the skins, then plunge them into ice water. Remove the tomatoes' cores and slip off the skins. Remove the seeds and chop the flesh.

In a heavy saucepot, heat the oil over medium-high heat. Add the chicken and the garlic cloves. Cook the chicken for 2 minutes on each side, or until golden brown. Scatter the onions over the chicken and cook for 2 to 3 minutes, or until the onions are softened.

Add the tomatoes, wine, bay leaf, and thyme and continue cooking for 15 minutes. Remove the garlic cloves, and peel and chop them. Mash the garlic to a paste. Return the mashed garlic to the saucepot and stir to combine. Cover the pot, and cook for 5 minutes longer. Season with salt and pepper. Remove the bay leaf and serve.

$\mathcal{M}$arinated $\mathcal{S}$hrimp $\mathcal{K}$ebabs

Makes 4 servings

We decided to spare you The Clever Cleaver Brothers' poem, but we didn't want to leave out their easy recipe for this excellent grilled dish. Here's a "clever" tip: Soak the wooden skewers in water for at least 1 hour prior to use. This will keep them from burning on the grill.

$\mathcal{B}irthdays$
~❦~

Tell about some of your happiest birthday party memories.

Regis: Joy loved giving birthday parties for our two girls. We had a very large backyard and the climate in Los Angeles made it possible to have wonderful outdoor parties and there was plenty of space for the kids to play games. Every year the parties seemed to get bigger. The kids were crazy about the Muppets, so Joy found the closest thing to a Muppets' show, with a Cookie Monster cake that was so blue everyone was afraid to eat it. It was Jennifer's most memorable party.

Kathie Lee: The first birthday that comes to mind is a recent one. I'd given birth to Cassidy on August 2nd. Then, on August 10th, Frank said, "You've got to come to New York. We'll bring the baby, we'll bring everybody. We'll spend the night in the city, because you've got to meet with the Disney people about a project. They know you just had a baby, but they're only in town for one day."

I thought it was pretty weird timing, but I said OK. So I took Cassidy, who was only eight days old, and Cody, and we went to New

---

1/2 cup olive oil

1 cup rice wine vinegar

2 tablespoons fresh or dried tarragon leaves

2 tablespoons Dijon-style mustard

1 tablespoon honey

Few dashes of Angostura aromatic bitters

2 large green peppers, cut into 1-inch cubes

1 large Spanish onion, cut into 1-inch cubes

16 large shrimp

1 can (20 ounces) pineapple chunks

(continued)

York. When I opened the door to my apartment there were about 60 of my friends standing there. It was a surprise fortieth birthday party for me.

I was a little angry with Frank because I hadn't really done my hair and makeup. But I was so happy to share my new baby with everyone, and so happy to see people. You know, in the last couple of months of your pregnancy, you just hide. I wasn't thrilled about myself then. I had been in premature labor for two weeks before the baby was born, and I hadn't wanted to see anybody. So the surprise party was kind of fun. I felt I was coming out of a dungeon and back into the world.

Kathie Lee, have you given any special birthday parties for Cody?

Kathie Lee: The last couple of years it's worked out beautifully, because I've been working at Disney World on Cody's birthday. We had his second and third birthdays there, and I don't know any better place in the world for a child's birthday party. We've taken along Cody's two best friends, Cailin and Robbie, who are my nanny's niece and nephew, and it's always lots of fun. The kids ride on the rides and then we go to the '50s diner at the MGM Disney Studios and have a big cake.

At least 2 hours before you will be grilling, stir together the marinade ingredients. (This will give the flavors time to blend.) In a shallow glass dish that is large enough to hold 4 skewers, stir together the oil, vinegar, tarragon, mustard, honey, and bitters.

Immerse the peppers and onion in boiling water for about 1 minute, or until they are softened slightly.

Peel and devein the shrimp. To devein the shrimp, using the point of a sharp knife, make a shallow cut down the center back (the curved side) of each shrimp and remove the dark vein. Rinse away any bits of the vein that remain. Butterfly each shrimp by deepening the cut made for deveining, cutting almost, but not quite, through to the underside. Open each shrimp like a book.

Thread one of the opened shrimp on a skewer, and follow it with alternating pieces of pepper, onion, and pineapple. Repeat twice, ending with a shrimp. Repeat with the remaining 3 skewers.

Place the kebabs in the marinade and refrigerate for 2 hours, basting the kebabs occasionally.

Using a paper towel, lightly rub a little vegetable oil on a grill or broiler pan. Position the grill or broiler pan 5 to 6 inches away from the heat source and cook the kebabs for about 3 minutes on each side, or until the shrimp are cooked through, basting frequently with the marinade.

$\mathcal{B}$lueberry $\mathcal{C}$obbler

Makes 8 servings

 When cookbook authors Linda and Fred Griffith entertain, they always have one item that evokes a "gee whiz" response. Even if the rest of the meal is very simple, that special dish seems to make the whole meal shine. They like to prepare this recipe in the morning and bake it later so that it can be served very warm, which Linda says is "simply heavenly." Gee whiz, we'd like to go to one of their parties!

2 cups plus 2 tablespoons granulated sugar, divided
2 cups all-purpose flour, divided
2 teaspoons grated lemon peel
8 cups fresh blueberries
2 teaspoons baking powder
1/2 teaspoon salt
1/2 cup (1 stick) unsalted (sweet) butter, softened
1 large egg plus 1 large egg yolk, lightly beaten
2 pints vanilla ice cream

Preheat the oven to 375°F. Butter a 3-quart baking dish.

In a large bowl, stir together 1 1/2 cups of the sugar, 1/4 cup of the flour, and the lemon peel. Add the blueberries and toss lightly to coat. Pour the mixture into the prepared baking dish.

In another bowl, stir together 1/2 cup of the sugar, the remaining 1 3/4 cups flour, the baking powder, and 1/2 teaspoon of salt. Stir in the butter until the mixture resembles coarse crumbs. Stir in the egg mixture until the dough holds together.

Distribute spoonfuls of the dough over the top of the blueberries and sprinkle the surface evenly with the remaining 2 tablespoons of sugar.

Bake for 35 minutes. Serve warm with vanilla ice cream.

Chapter 10

Fantastic Fourth of July and Other Summertime Sensations

···············~❦~···············

B oth Regis and Kathie Lee like entertaining in the
summertime. The warm weather provides opportunities
for outdoor parties, and backyards, patios, and porches give
everyone more space for entertaining. Backyards can usually
accommodate croquet, volleyball, horseshoes, and other outdoor
games, and even if you don't have your very own pools and tennis
courts, as Regis and Kathie Lee do, you can always take
advantage of parks and recreational areas. Wide open spaces are
wonderful for entertaining kids, and you don't have to worry about
anything getting broken.

As you might guess, this chapter is filled with grilled foods and recipes that make use of summer's fresh produce. Some recipes, such as the barbecue sauces from restaurateur Lola, lend themselves to casual, finger-lickin' eating, while others could be elegantly presented with your finest china on the patio.

Summertime Entertaining Tips

~§~

- Use wooden baskets filled with fresh summer produce as centerpieces. For instance, a big basket of just-washed strawberries looks gorgeous, and the berries are delicious for snacking.

- Look for inexpensive material to use as outdoor tablecloths. If you need to cover more than one table, use the same color theme throughout—maybe using reverse prints. Use clip-type clothespins to weight down the edges of the tablecloth or to secure it at the corners.

- Fill a basket with picnic essentials so that you are ready to pick up and picnic at a moment's notice. Some items to include: a tablecloth, paper plates, cups, napkins, utensils, wet wipes, trash bags, sunscreen, insect repellent, and a disposable camera.

- Potted plants grouped together in the center of the table make an easy centerpiece. Or put a small potted plant at each place setting—cherry tomato or pepper plants, perhaps.

- To be ecologically friendly when you picnic, invest in sturdy, reusable plastic plates, cups, and utensils. Use cloth napkins. Tote everything home in a big bag or box for washing.

- Bandannas make great napkins and wash wonderfully well.

- To add elegance to a patio party, cover a picnic table with a beautiful tablecloth and then set the table with your finest china and silver. Create extra dazzle by stringing white Christmas lights in trees and bushes.

- Create a fruit flag for a patriotic and healthy seasonal dessert. Slice watermelon and jicama (a Southwestern root vegetable with a slightly sweet taste and applelike crunch) into strips that are 3 inches long by 1/2 inch tall by 1/2 inch thick. Use a shallow rectangular tray or serving dish to hold your "flag." Create a 2-inch-wide stripe of watermelon along the bottom edge of the tray. Follow with a stripe of jicama and repeat until three-fourths of the tray is covered. Continue making stripes to the top of the tray on the right-hand side to resemble the American flag. Fill the left-hand corner with blueberries. Cut a few pointed stars out of jicama and arrange them on top of the blueberries.

- Or make a cake that looks like a flag. Frost a rectangular sheet cake with white frosting. Add rows of raspberries to create stripes. Arrange blueberries in the upper left-hand corner, leaving some of the white showing through to create stars.

- Use blue curacão to make patriotic margaritas or daiquiris.

- Drizzle blueberry and raspberry purées onto white plates in an attractive design and serve your desert on them.

When is your favorite time for entertaining?

~ℰ~

Regis: Our country house lends itself to entertaining in the summertime. We have a large veranda which we use all summer long as our dining room, weather permitting. We use the outdoor grill for everything. We are tennis fanatics so most of our entertaining revolves around our tennis matches. I bought the house because the grounds are so lovely.

Kathie Lee: I love summertime entertaining. We love to play tennis and have cookouts and family events. The kids can swim in our pool while the parents play tennis. It's a fun family time. Frank mans the grill.

Regis and Hal Linden prepare a scrumptious dish.

How do you celebrate
the Fourth of July?

~ ℰ ~

Regis: The Fourth of July was more of an event for us when we lived in California. We'd celebrate on the beach because they have fireworks there and that was terrific. When we moved to New York City, we would always go on the Hudson River where the Macy's spectacular takes place. We've been on a variety of boats, including Malcolm Forbes's yacht. On the boats there were usually sandwiches and hamburgers—a typical American menu to go along with the fireworks.

What do you serve
when you entertain?

~ ℰ ~

Kathie Lee: We really don't serve fancy, ornate foods. Our friends aren't fancy or fussy people so we don't serve fussy foods. I don't care how pretty a dish looks if it doesn't taste delicious. Sometimes you see these magnificent buffets that look just gorgeous. Then you taste the food and it's full of gel to preserve it so that it will last a long time and look good. I'm not interested in that. I want the food to be as good as it looks.

I'm a meat and potatoes kind of gal and Frank is a meat and potatoes kind of guy. We like healthy food but it has to be simple. Very often, at our home in Connecticut in the summertime, we serve a big seafood salad that is my own recipe. We probably have that three times a week during the summertime. Or we'll grill swordfish and serve it with a baked potato and a big head of broccoli. We are very big salad eaters. We're trying to get Cody to eat salad. Even if there is a piece of lettuce on a turkey sandwich, he'll say, "Mommy, take the salad out." He doesn't want anything green. We're battling that right now.

Petra's Shrimp, Avocado, and Tomato Pies

Makes 4 servings

J anos Wilder, chef and owner of a restaurant bearing his name in Tucson, Arizona, demonstrated this stylish recipe on a hot summer day. His 90-seat restaurant is located in an old adobe, a historic landmark that was owned in the 1800s by a colorful and prominent citizen named Hiram Stevens and his wife, Petra. Janos named this contemporary recipe after Petra because the ingredients represent her Mexican heritage.

To make round-shaped molded recipes, many chefs use the ring molds that are available in restaurant supply stores. Janos suggested a helpful tip for creating individual molds for his layered recipe: Use four 6 1/2- to 7-ounce tuna cans with both ends removed. The recipe works well either as a first course or as part of a light lunch. To give the pies a more dramatic appearance, stand three pieces of fresh chive on top of each serving. When asked for great entertaining tips, Janos responded, "Invite Regis to your party!"

LAYERED MOLDS
16 medium shrimp
2 medium, ripe avocados, peeled, pitted, and diced
1 bunch fresh cilantro leaves
1/4 cup freshly squeezed lime juice
20 red and/or yellow cherry tomatoes, cut in half

TOMATO VINAIGRETTE
4 medium tomatoes, diced
6 tablespoons olive oil
2 tablespoons balsamic vinegar
Whole or chopped fresh chives, for garnish (optional)

To Make the Layered Molds: Peel and devein the shrimp. To devein the shrimp, using the point of a sharp knife, make a shallow cut down the center back (the curved side) of each shrimp, and remove the dark vein. Rinse away any bits of the vein that remain.

In a steamer basket over boiling water, steam the shrimp for 2 to 3 minutes, or until they are pink and cooked through. Rinse the shrimp with cold water and drain.

In a large bowl, gently toss together the avocado, cilantro, and lime juice.

Place a small ring mold (or a 6 1/2- to 7-ounce tuna can with top and bottom removed) in the center of each of 4 salad plates. Arrange 4 shrimp in the bottom of each mold. Spoon the avocado mixture over the top of the shrimp and gently press down. Arrange the cherry tomato halves on top.

To Make the Tomato Vinaigrette: In a large bowl, stir together the diced tomatoes, oil, and vinegar.

Spoon the tomato mixture around the base of the molds and sprinkle chives over the tomato vinaigrette. Carefully remove the molds, preserving the "pie" shapes, and serve.

Chilled Fresh Pea Soup with Rosemary Cream and Bacon

Makes 4 to 6 servings

C hef/owner Daniel Boulud of Manhattan's Restaurant Daniel prepared the following recipe for one of his favorite soups for a summer lunch. A thermos filled with this chilled soup would be a stylish addition to any picnic or barbecue.

FRESH PEA SOUP

2 quarts of chicken stock or broth
1 1/2 teaspoons olive oil
1 cup chopped sweet onion
1/2 cup chopped celery
1 ounce sliced bacon
1 sprig of fresh rosemary or 1/2 teaspoon dried rosemary
  leaves
5 cups shelled fresh peas

ROSEMARY CREAM

1/4 cup heavy (whipping) cream
1 sprig of fresh rosemary or 1/2 teaspoon dried rosemary
  leaves
1 garlic clove, finely chopped
Salt and pepper to taste
Croutons, for garnish (optional)
Additional chopped cooked bacon, for garnish (optional)

To Make the Soup: In a large saucepot, bring the chicken stock to a boil. Reduce the heat and keep the stock warm.

In another large saucepot, heat the olive oil over medium heat. Cook the onion, celery, bacon, and rosemary for 5 to 7 minutes, or until the vegetables are softened but not browned.

Stir in the peas and cook for 2 to 3 minutes. Pour in the hot chicken stock. Bring the mixture to a boil and cook for 5 minutes.

Cool the soup by placing the pot in a very large bowl or pot that is filled with ice water.'

When the soup is cool, discard the bacon and rosemary. In a blender or food processor, in several batches, process the soup until smooth.

Strain the soup and refrigerate until cold.

To Make the Rosemary Cream: In a small saucepan, combine the cream, rosemary, garlic, salt, and pepper. Bring the mixture to a boil and boil gently for 5 to 8 minutes, or until slightly thickened. Strain the mixture and cool.

Ladle the chilled soup into chilled bowls. Drizzle some of the rosemary cream into each bowl. Sprinkle the tops of the bowls with croutons and chopped bacon, if desired.

Kathie Lee looking as elegant as ever.

Tomato Vinaigrette

 omatoes are at their finest in the summer, and this recipe from *Jeremiah Tower's New American Classics* is hard to beat. As the esteemed chef/owner of Stars restaurants in San Francisco, Napa Valley, and Palo Alto, Jeremiah tries to use fruits and vegetables when they are in season. In fact, he says it can become an obsession! Grow your own fresh herbs in a garden or window box so you'll always have a fragrant supply on hand to create this versatile recipe. On "Live," Jeremiah tossed it with linguine and garnished it with the flowers of fresh herbs and nasturtiums.

Tomato Vinaigrette can be served on any warm pasta, in pasta salads, and over hot or chilled asparagus. It is equally good as a condiment with grilled fish, chicken, and meat, and as a topping for grilled garlic bread. Jeremiah suggests this recipe when you are short on time. For instance, if you are expecting dinner guests after a day of work, put a big pot of water on to boil for blanching the tomatoes and cooking the pasta, take a shower, and pour yourself a glass of white wine. By the time you are refreshed from your shower, the water will be boiling, and you can easily pull together a delightful meal for your guests.

3 medium tomatoes (try a combination of red and yellow tomatoes)
1/4 cup coarsely chopped fresh herbs, such as basil, marjoram, parsley, tarragon, thyme, or fennel
1/4 cup freshly squeezed lemon juice or vinegar
2 large shallots, peeled and coarsely chopped
1 cup extra-virgin olive oil
Salt and freshly ground black pepper to taste

In a large saucepan, bring water to a boil. Meanwhile, remove the cores from the tomatoes. Place the tomatoes in the water for about 5 seconds—do not overcook them, or they will turn to mush. Plunge them immediately into a bath of ice and water for about 30 seconds. Peel off the skins and discard.

Cut each tomato across the "equator"—(do not cut down through the stem or you will seal off some of the seed chambers). Hold the tomato halves cut side down and squeeze out the seeds. Dice the tomatoes and put them in a strainer over a bowl to drain.

Just before you are ready to serve the sauce, combine the tomatoes with the remaining ingredients. The sauce should be loosely mixed and not an emulsion.

Kathie Lee's Chesapeake Bay Memories

~ℓ~

When we lived by the Chesapeake Bay in Maryland, we'd have crab feasts that would last all day long. We'd cover a big long picnic table with newspaper, my daddy would steam the crabs and season them, and then we'd eat them. The grownups would drink good old Maryland beer—it was called National Beer and was brewed in Baltimore, but it's no longer available. It was a real Maryland kind of event. After we'd eaten our fill of crabs, we'd play volleyball and other games. A couple of hours later, we'd come back to the table and eat some more crabs. We could eat literally bushels of crabs.

This wasn't like going to the fish store and getting a nice little tin of freshly picked crab. It took us a long, long time because we had to pick them ourselves. After we finished, we'd just douse ourselves with lemon juice. I became and remain to this day one of the great crab pickers of all time—it's a talent of mine that nauseates Frank!

~ℓ~

W hen it comes to barbecuing, it's hard to beat Lola Yvonne Bell, co-owner of New York City's Lolabelle Restaurant. Following are four of her favorite recipes for glazes and sauces for grilling. Use them, according to your personal taste, on meats, poultry, and fish. When asked for "entertaining" tips, Lola's response is "Pray." We think it's Lola's sunny personality that helps make sure all her guests feel welcomed.

HONEY GLAZE
Makes about 1 cup of glaze

1 cup orange juice
1 cup red wine
1/4 cup honey
1/4 dark soy sauce
1/2 teaspoon red wine vinegar

In a medium saucepan, combine the orange juice and wine. Bring the mixture to a boil and continue to boil until the mixture is reduced to 1/2 cup. Remove the pan from the heat and whisk in the remaining ingredients. Use the mixture to baste poultry or meat as you grill it. As a finishing touch, brush the glaze onto the meat.

SWEET AND SPICY MEAT GLAZE
Makes about 2 1/4 cups

1 cup firmly packed brown sugar
1 cup white vinegar
1/2 cup golden raisins
3 garlic cloves, finely chopped
1 tablespoon finely chopped gingerroot
1 teaspoon cayenne pepper
1 teaspoon salt

In the container of a food processor or blender, process all the ingredients together until smooth. Use this glaze as a marinade or brush it on meat just before you are ready to serve it.

LOLA'S BARBECUE SAUCE
Makes about 4 cups

2 cups puréed tomatoes
1/2 cup mango chutney
1/2 cup Dijon-style mustard
1/2 cup bourbon
1/2 cup strained freshly squeezed lemon juice
1/4 cup firmly packed brown sugar
1 Scotch bonnet pepper, seeded and finely chopped, or 1
    teaspoon cayenne pepper
1 teaspoon salt

In a medium saucepan, combine all the ingredients. Heat the mixture over medium-high heat until it comes to a boil, stirring occasionally. Reduce the heat, cover partially, and simmer for 20 minutes. Use as you would any other barbecue sauce.

BLACK JACK BARBECUE SAUCE
Makes about 5 1/2 cups of sauce

This all-purpose barbecue sauce was prepared on the sidewalk outside the "Live" studio as the lead-in recipe to "Barbecue Week." Lola Yvonne Bell says she received inspiration for this recipe, as for most of the food she serves, from her mother and grandmother.

1/4 cup vegetable oil
2 cups finely chopped onions
1 1/2 tablespoons finely chopped garlic
1/2 cup cider vinegar
1 cup brewed black coffee
1 cup Worcestershire sauce
1 cup tomato ketchup
1/2 cup firmly packed brown sugar

(continued)

1 small chipotle pepper, finely chopped, or cayenne pepper to
   taste
1/2 teaspoon salt

In a medium saucepan, heat the oil over medium-high heat. Add the onions, garlic, and vinegar and cook until all the liquid has evaporated. Add the remaining ingredients and cook for 10 minutes to blend the flavors, stirring frequently. Use the sauce when you barbecue meats or poultry.

Oriental Grilled Chicken Salad

Makes 2 to 4 servings

During those dog days of summer, Chef Tell comes to the rescue with the perfect recipe for a chicken pasta salad.

MARINADE AND DRESSING

1/2 cup teriyaki sauce
1/4 cup sesame oil
1 tablespoon finely chopped gingerroot
1 tablespoon finely chopped garlic
Salt and pepper to taste

CHICKEN SALAD

4 boneless, skinless chicken breast halves
1 tablespoon olive oil
1 pound of egg fettuccine, freshly cooked according to
   package directions
1 medium carrot, cut into julienne strips (about 1/2 cup)
1 medium celery stalk, cut into julienne strips (about 1/2
   cup)
4 to 5 scallions, cut into flowers for garnish (optional)

To Make the Marinade and Dressing: In a small bowl, mix together the teriyaki sauce, sesame oil, gingerroot, garlic, salt, and pepper until combined. Divide the mixture in half.

Using a meat mallet, pound the chicken breasts to flatten them slightly. Let the chicken stand for a few minutes in half of the teriyaki mixture.

You can either grill, broil, or sauté the chicken breasts.

To Grill or Broil the Chicken: Using a paper towel, lightly rub a little of the olive oil on the grill or broiler pan. Position the grill or broiler 5 to 6 inches away from the heat source. Remove the chicken from the teriyaki mixture and discard the marinade. Grill or broil the chicken for 5 to 7 minutes on each side, or until cooked through.

(continued)

To Sauté the Chicken Breasts: In a large skillet, heat the olive oil over medium-high heat. Cook the chicken breasts for 5 to 7 minutes on each side, or until cooked through.

Cut the chicken into 1/2-inch-wide strips. Transfer the fettuccine to a warm serving platter. Pour the remaining teriyaki mixture over the pasta. Add the carrots and celery and toss to combine. Adjust the seasonings. Arrange the chicken on top of the pasta. Garnish with scallion flowers, if desired.

Kathie Lee's Seafood Salad

Makes 6 servings

T his refreshing recipe from Kathie Lee is one of her favorite summertime meals. She serves it on a bed of lettuce, accompanied by a wedge of cantaloupe or fresh berries, and hot French bread. Kathie Lee likes this with lots of freshly squeezed lemon juice, and adds fresh Maryland crabmeat whenever it's available.

1 pound cooked shrimp, cut into 1/2-inch pieces
1 pound sea legs (seafood chunks), cut into bite-size pieces or torn into shreds
3/4 to 1 cup good-quality mayonnaise
2 celery stalks, diced
About 1/2 cup finely chopped parsley
Juice of 1 to 2 lemons to taste
Salt and pepper to taste
Lettuce leaves

In a large bowl, stir together the shrimp, sea legs, and mayonnaise until combined. Stir in the celery, parsley, lemon juice, salt, and pepper. Cover and refrigerate to allow the flavors to blend. Just before serving, adjust the seasonings, adding more lemon juice and salt and pepper to taste. Serve on a bed of lettuce leaves.

Salmon on a Bed of Spinach Salad

Makes 1 serving

Try this dish as a special lunch to entertain yourself. It was created by Chef Daniel Boulud of Manhattan's highly esteemed Restaurant Daniel.

3 tablespoons olive oil, divided
1 (6-ounce) skinless, boneless salmon fillet
1 lemon
1/4 cup diced fresh tomato
1 1/2 teaspoons chopped chives
1/4 pound tender raw spinach leaves
2 white mushrooms, caps removed and cut into julienne
   strips
1 tablespoon chopped fresh cilantro leaves

In a medium skillet, heat 1/2 tablespoon of the olive oil. Add the salmon and cook until lightly browned on both sides. Keep warm.

Grate the peel from the lemon. Juice the lemon and chop the flesh.

In a small saucepan, stir together the grated lemon peel, lemon juice, lemon flesh, tomato, the remaining 2 1/2 tablespoons of olive oil, and the chives. Stir over medium heat for 2 to 4 minutes, or until warmed through.

Arrange the spinach on a plate and top with the salmon. Spoon the dressing over the salmon. Sprinkle the mushrooms and the chopped cilantro leaves over the top.

Tips for Entertaining from Jeffrey Nathan

~&~

*J*effrey and his wife, Alison, are both trained chefs with some great ideas on how to entertain successfully at home. Of course, like all good party givers, they recommend having everything planned ahead of time except for last-minute warming, so that you can enjoy spending time with your guests.

Some of their other clever suggestions:

- As an added attraction, leave an instant lottery ticket at each place setting. This is an inexpensive party favor with great possibilities.

- Hire or enlist someone (a neighbor or friend) to help clear the dishes and straighten the kitchen. You'll have more time to enjoy your company and your kitchen won't be a wreck for everyone to see.

- If your guests are whole families, provide entertainment for the children at dessert time. By then, the children are generally bored and the parents are in a mood to relax.

$\mathcal{P}$apaya $\mathcal{C}$hicken with $\mathcal{F}$resh $\mathcal{F}$ruit $\mathcal{C}$ompote

Makes 2 servings

Chef Jeffrey Nathan from the New Deal Restaurant and Garden in New York City prepared this fresh-tasting chicken breast dish that is accompanied by a spicy, fruity salsa. You can adjust the salsa according to the fruits and vegetables currently in season; on "Live," Jeffrey used melon, strawberries, and apple. He also likes to prepare this recipe with chopped pineapple, and sometimes adds a small amount of chopped red bell pepper for a bright touch of color. Jeffrey's favorite accompaniments: steamed white rice, a fresh green vegetable, and a tossed green salad.

2 boneless, skinless chicken breast halves
All-purpose flour for dredging the chicken
2 tablespoons olive oil
1 papaya, peeled, seeded, and diced
3 tablespoons rice wine vinegar
3 tablespoons white wine
2 tablespoons butter
1 1/2 cups berries and chopped fruits in season
1 jalapeño pepper, seeded and finely chopped
1 small red onion, diced
2 tablespoons balsamic vinegar
Chopped fresh cilantro and fresh mint leaves to taste
Salt and pepper to taste

Dip the chicken breasts in the flour to lightly coat both sides; shake off any excess.

In a large skillet, heat the oil over medium-high heat. Cook the chicken breasts and papaya together, turning the chicken once, for 10 to 15 minutes, or until the chicken is cooked through and lightly browned.

(continued)

Add the rice wine vinegar and wine and bring quickly to a boil. Remove the skillet from the heat and stir in the butter. Transfer the chicken breasts and sauce to a plate and keep warm.

In a large bowl, toss together the fruit, jalapeño pepper, and red onion. Stir in the balsamic vinegar, cilantro, mint, salt, and pepper. Serve this salsa alongside the chicken breasts.

Pointers on Papayas

~ ℰ ~

Botanically, the pear-shaped papaya is a berry, one of many that hang from the branches of a tropical tree that grows from seed to twenty feet high in about eighteen months. Most of the papayas we consume in North America are grown in Hawaii.

Papayas that are fully ripe are golden yellow in color. A papaya that is solid green will not ripen well, so look for papayas that have at least a little yellow in their skins. Let them ripen at room temperature. If you want papayas to ripen more quickly, place them in a paper bag.

Like melons, papayas have seeds located in a cavity in the center of the fruit. Cut them lengthwise and scoop out the seeds. A splash of freshly squeezed lime juice enlivens the sweet, slightly bland flavor of this fruit. Try them at breakfast in place of melon. For an easy tropical dessert, serve each papaya half with a scoop of vanilla ice cream in the cavity.

Ratatouille

With this recipe, Chef Tell shows us how to take advantage of summer's bounty when it is at its peak. On "Live," Chef Tell served the ratatouille over pasta, but he also suggested using it as you would salsa. He likes to arrange chicken or fish on top of a base of this classic vegetable mixture. Ratatouille can be served warm, at room temperature as a side-dish vegetable, or cold as a salad. It's well suited for entertaining because it tastes even better the day after it is made, as the flavors start to blend together.

1/4 cup vegetable or olive oil
1 onion, peeled and cut into thin slices
2 pounds eggplant, peeled and cut into thin slices
4 zucchini, trimmed and cut into thin slices
2 tomatoes, peeled and seeded
2 garlic cloves, peeled and finely chopped
Salt and pepper to taste
1/4 cup chopped fresh parsley

In a large skillet, heat the oil over medium-high heat. Add the onion and cook for about 5 minutes, or until the onion is softened but not browned.

Add the eggplant, zucchini, tomatoes, garlic, salt, and pepper. Cook for 10 to 20 minutes, or until the vegetables soften to the texture you prefer. Sprinkle the parsley over the mixture just before serving.

$\mathcal{G}$elman's $\mathcal{G}$arden-fresh $\mathcal{P}$asta $\mathcal{S}$auce

Makes 4 to 6 servings

This is one of Executive Producer Michael Gelman's favorite recipes. He created it using some of the fresh produce from the prolific garden of his weekend house on Long Island. This pasta sauce is almost like salsa or gazpacho, he says, and it's a great recipe to make early in the day and refrigerate. After you have spent the rest of the day in the sun, you can have this flavorful sauce all ready to add to freshly cooked pasta. Michael likes to serve it with a tossed green salad dressed with balsamic vinegar and extra-virgin olive oil. He accompanies this simple meal with a crusty loaf of peasant bread and cold, light white wine.

1 pound fusilli pasta
1 cup finely chopped cucumbers (peeled and seeded, if
    desired)
1/2 pound goat cheese, divided
1/2 cup extra-virgin olive oil
1/4 cup balsamic vinegar
4 garlic cloves, crushed
10 fresh basil leaves
1 jalapeño pepper (seeded, if desired)
2 pounds Italian plum tomatoes or yellow tomatoes, coarsely
    chopped
Salt and pepper to taste
Tabasco sauce (optional)

Bring a large pot of salted water to a boil. Add the pasta and cook just until *al dente*. Drain thoroughly and keep warm.

In the container of a food processor fitted with the metal chopping blade, process the cucumbers, half of the goat cheese, the olive oil, vinegar, garlic, basil, and jalapeño pepper until smooth. Add the tomatoes and pulse just until the sauce is chunky. Crumble the remaining goat cheese into the sauce. Season with salt, pepper, and Tabasco, if desired. Serve the sauce over the fusilli.

End-of-the-Summer Pesto

Makes 6 servings

I f you plant an herb garden that includes basil and parsley, count on being rewarded with a harvest that enables you to make this excellent recipe from the Love Chef. Francis Anthony advises that in addition to going well on pasta, "a little pesto peps up broiled fish, ho-hum soup, and stews."

3 tablespoons unsalted (sweet) butter
2 tablespoons walnut meats
1 tablespoon pine nuts
1 garlic clove
1/4 teaspoon ground white pepper
1/4 teaspoon grated orange peel
Pinch of freshly grated nutmeg
1/2 cup freshly grated Parmesan cheese
2 cups loosely packed fresh basil leaves
1/4 cup loosely packed Italian parsley leaves
6 tablespoons olive oil
1 pound linguine

In the container of a food processor fitted with the metal chopping blade, combine the butter, walnuts, pine nuts, garlic, pepper, orange peel, and nutmeg. Process until smooth. With the processor running, gradually add the cheese, then the basil and parsley. Gradually add the oil and continue processing until the paste is smooth.

Bring a large pot of salted water to a boil. Add the linguine and cook just until *al dente*. Drain thoroughly and toss with the pesto sauce.

Peach Cobbler

Makes 4 to 6 servings

 Here, Chef Tell Erhardt works his special culinary magic with summer's fresh peaches. Serve this dessert in stemmed wineglasses and top each serving with a dollop of whipped cream or crème fraîche. Vanilla ice cream also goes remarkably well with peach cobbler.

FRUIT MIXTURE

4 cups sliced peaches
1/2 cup granulated sugar
1/2 cup plain bread crumbs
Grated peel and juice of 1 lemon
A few drops of cherry brandy

STREUSEL TOPPING

1 1/4 cups all-purpose flour
6 tablespoons granulated sugar
1/4 cup (1/2 stick) unsalted (sweet) butter
1/2 teaspoon vanilla extract
Dash of ground cinnamon
Dash of salt

Preheat the oven to 375°F. Butter a 1 1/2-quart baking dish.

To Make the Fruit Mixture: In a large bowl, mix together the peaches, sugar, bread crumbs, lemon peel, lemon juice, and cherry brandy. Place the mixture in the prepared dish.

To Make the Streusel Topping: In another bowl, using your fingertips, mix the streusel ingredients together until they form coarse crumbs.

Sprinkle the streusel mixture evenly over the top of the peach mixture in the dish.

Bake for 45 minutes, or until the topping is lightly browned.

Ice Cream Cherry Delights

Makes 4 servings

These delicious sundaes should be made with homemade vanilla ice cream. Chef Daniel Boulud of New York City's Restaurant Daniel developed this recipe to make use of cherries when they are at their finest in the summer.

1 pound fresh sweet cherries
3 tablespoons maple syrup
Juice of 1 lemon
1 pint homemade vanilla ice cream
2 tablespoons sliced toasted almonds
Fresh mint leaves
Grated orange peel
Whipped heavy cream
Ground cinnamon

Cut the cherries in half and remove the pits.

In a medium saucepan, heat the maple syrup over medium heat. Add the cherries and cook for 2 to 3 minutes. Stir in the lemon juice.

Place a 1/2-cup scoop of the ice cream in each of 4 dessert dishes. Spoon the hot cherry mixture over the ice cream. Decorate the top of each sundae with the almonds, mint leaves, orange peel, whipped cream, and a sprinkling of cinnamon. Serve immediately.

Martha Stewart's Blueberry Pie

Makes 1 deep 11-inch double-crust pie

When Martha Stewart makes blueberry pie, she doesn't add spices that might detract from the fresh taste of the blueberries. Here's her recipe featuring leaves cut from pastry and arranged attractively on top of the pie. The crust is then glazed with an egg-yolk-and-cream mixture and sprinkled with sugar, which makes it glisten.

Pâte Brisée (recipe follows) for an 11-inch double-crust pie, chilled

3 pints fresh blueberries, washed, drained, and picked over

1 cup plus 1 tablespoon granulated sugar, divided

1/3 to 1/2 cup sifted all-purpose flour

1 tablespoon unsalted (sweet) butter, cut into small pieces

1/2 cup heavy (whipping) cream

1 large egg

Preheat the oven to 400°F. Lightly butter or spray with vegetable cooking spray a 2-inch-deep 11-inch tart pan. Place the tart pan on a parchment-lined baking sheet.

On a lightly floured board, roll out half of the pâte brisée into a circle that is large enough to fit the prepared tart pan. Place the pastry in the tart pan and press it into the bottom edge and along the side. Trim the pastry using scissors or a sharp paring knife, or by rolling a rolling pin across the top of the pan. (Martha often cuts the pastry an inch or so higher than the edge of the tart pan and tucks this overhang to the inside of the pan for extra height and reinforcement.) Chill the pastry-lined pan until ready to use.

On a lightly floured board, roll out the remaining pastry to a thickness of 1/8 inch and cut out leaf shapes using a sharp paring knife. Make the veins of the leaves by pressing the back of the knife into each leaf. Transfer the leaves to a parchment-lined or water-sprayed baking sheet, cover, and refrigerate until ready to use.

Put the blueberries in a large bowl and sprinkle with 1 cup of the sugar, the flour, and the butter. Gently toss so that the berries are completely covered.

In a small bowl, stir together the cream and egg until combined. Brush the entire pastry crust (edge and bottom) with the egg glaze and pour the blueberries into the shell. Decoratively arrange the leaves on top of the fruit, covering it almost completely. Brush the leaves with the egg glaze and sprinkle with the remaining 1 tablespoon of sugar.

Bake the pie for 50 minutes, or until the blueberry juices have bubbled and thickened. Let the pie cool completely on a wire rack before cutting.

(continued)

Kathie Lee gets a kick out of Regis's antics on the set.

PÂTE BRISÉE

This recipe makes enough crust for the preceding pie, or two 8-to-10-inch tarts or single-crust pies, or one 8-to-10-inch double-crust pie, or 12 2 1/2-to-3-inch tartlets. For best results, make sure that all of the ingredients are cold.

2 1/2 cups all-purpose flour
1 teaspoon salt
1 teaspoon granulated sugar (optional)
1 cup (2 sticks) cold unsalted (sweet) butter, cut into small
    pieces
1/4 to 1/2 cup ice water

Put the flour, salt, and sugar in the container of a food processor fitted with the metal chopping blade. Add the pieces of butter and process for approximately 10 seconds, or just until the mixture resembles coarse meal. (To mix by hand, combine the dry ingredients in a large bowl. Using a pastry blender or 2 knives used scissors-fashion, cut in the butter until the mixture resembles coarse meal.)

Drop by drop, add the ice water through the feed tube with the machine running, just until the dough holds together without being wet or sticky; do not process more than 30 seconds. Test the dough at this point by squeezing a small amount together. If it is crumbly, add a bit more water.

Turn the dough out onto a large piece of plastic wrap. Press the dough into a flat circle with your fists. (This makes rolling the dough easier than if the pastry is chilled as a ball.) Wrap the dough in the plastic wrap and chill for at least 1 hour.

$\mathcal{P}$early $\mathcal{P}$eaches

Makes 4 to 6 servings

 indy MacDonald, segment producer for "Live," advises that if your peaches are hard and you don't have time to let them ripen, you can put them one at a time into the microwave oven, and cook on High for 20 to 30 seconds. Microwaving also makes them easier to peel. When Cindy entertains, she likes to pay special attention to her selection of music. Her parties often feature homemade pasta sauce or homemade pizza, with this recipe as a fitting finale.

4 cups peeled, sliced fresh *ripe* peaches
3/4 cup granulated sugar (or to taste)
1/4 cup Minute Tapioca (use a little less for a looser
    consistency)
1 to 2 tablespoons freshly squeezed lemon juice
3/4 teaspoon ground cinnamon
Homemade whipped cream, vanilla ice cream, or vanilla
    yogurt (optional)
Pinch of grated nutmeg

In a 1 1/2-quart ovenproof baking dish, combine the peaches, sugar, tapioca, lemon juice, and cinnamon. Let stand for 15 minutes while you preheat the oven to 350°F. Bake the mixture for 30 minutes. Shut the oven off and leave the baking dish in the oven until the peaches are tender and the tapioca looks like little see-through pearls. Serve warm or cold topped with whipped cream, ice cream, or yogurt and a sprinkling of nutmeg.

Chapter 11

Harvest Moon Celebration

·················· ∽℃∾ ··················

W hen Jack Frost pays his annual visit, it's time to pull
out all the stops and serve hearty foods that make use
of the season's bountiful harvest. For instance, Chef Scott Cohen
of Manhattan's Tatou serves up a delicious variation of
Old-Fashioned Vegetable Pot Pie. This recipe can easily be
adapted to make use of the best seasonal vegetables available.
Actress Crystal Carson likes to serve her special Nebraska-style
sandwiches—pockets of bread dough that are filled with beef,
cabbage, mushrooms, and onions. Sylvia Woods, of the soul-food
restaurant named for her in Harlem, serves her extra-special
Southern-style ribs. For dessert, try Chef Tell's Baked Apple
Dumplings.

Do you have costume parties
for Halloween?

~⟡~

Regis: Our friends in Los Angeles, Barry and Susan Glazer, used to have great Halloween parties. We would be dressed in costumes and sent on scavenger hunts that would last for hours. It was very cleverly done and everyone really got into a competitive spirit.

I remember when my daughter JJ was about two or three years old,

---

Adding a Festive Fall
Feeling to Your Party

~⟡~

- Line the walk to your house with *luminarias*. To create them, put sand in the bottom of small paper bags. Insert votive candle in each bag. To create extra interest, cut out half-moon shapes around the top edge of the bag for the candle to glow through, or use pinking shears to trim around the top edge.

- Check the lunar calendar and schedule your party for the evening of a full moon.

- For a homespun centerpiece, fill a big basket with jars of homemade jams, jellies, and preserves. Line the basket with fall leaves and add other seasonal items such as apples, miniature pumpkins, and gourds. Not only have you created a beautiful display, but each guest gets to take home a jar of your homemade preserves. Make sure to decorate each jar with a fall theme, perhaps using labels with a leaf motif. Cover each jar with a calico jar topper. With a piece of jute twine, tie on a card with the recipe, so that your guests can make their own preserves.

---

she dressed up as Caspar the Ghost. She thought she was going to *terrify* everybody—it was really cute. I helped Caspar the Ghost trick or treat, and nobody batted an eye.

Kathie Lee: We thought we might hold a Halloween party this summer because the weather is so bad in October. Last year we put up a tent, but it was still too cold, so we might do better this year doing it early when it's still warm out. Cody is in ten to fifteen different outfits every day, so what's the difference! Every day of the year is Halloween for him.

- Serve your favorite punch or mulled cider as "Harvest Moonshine." In fact, this could be the theme for your party. On the invitations, you could invite people to a Harvest Moonshine party.

- Tie napkins with a piece of raffia or twine and insert a small branch of yellow and red bittersweet berries.

- Give your party a cowboy theme. Have a hayrack ride, hold a square dance, or give country-and-Western dance lessons. Stack bales of hay on your porch, and decorate with cactus to add authenticity to your get-together.

- Hollow out a large pumpkin to serve as a soup tureen for thick soups or stews. Serve the soup in smaller, hollowed-out pumpkins, complete with their lids. Small pumpkins also work well as seasonal holders for dips.

- Antique thread spools of varying sizes make attractive candlesticks. You can add pumpkins and gourds for a seasonal table setting.

- Cut spice or sugar cookies into leaf shapes, perhaps using real leaves as guides.

- Hold a scavenger hunt to look for different species of leaves. Provide a guidebook or samples of the leaves in your area, and give a present to the person who finds the most varieties or the child who collects the prettiest-colored leaves.

Devilish Split Pea Soup

Makes 8 to 10 servings

Dressed as the devil, Love Chef Francis Anthony demonstrated a hearty soup for a special Halloween show on "Live." Regis, sporting a thin mustache, was dressed as Zorro. Kathie Lee was dressed as a French chambermaid. Actress Linda Blair joined the festivities on the set and got to sample the soup after it was cooked.

1 pound dried split green peas
6 cups chicken stock or broth
1 teaspoon hot pepper sauce
2 smoked ham hocks
2 cups low-fat milk
1 large onion, chopped
1 large potato, peeled and diced
2 bay leaves
1 1/2 teaspoons dried dill weed
1/2 teaspoon ground white pepper
Salt (optional)
Crushed red pepper flakes (optional)

In a large pot, combine all of the ingredients. Bring the mixture to a boil over medium-high heat. Reduce the heat and simmer for about 60 minutes, stirring occasionally.

Remove the ham hocks from the pot to a cutting board. Trim off the fat and the bone and discard. Cut the meat into thin slivers and add them to the pot. Cook for 30 to 60 minutes longer, until the soup is of the desired consistency.

Crawfish and Corn Maque Choux

Makes 10 to 12 side-dish servings

C hef Paul Prudhomme of K-Paul's Louisiana Kitchen in New Orleans is the author of several cookbooks—most recently, *Fork in the Road*—and a special favorite of Kathie Lee's. Serve this recipe with rice and Chef Paul's Bronzed Chicken Breasts (see page 126) for a delicious Louisiana-style meal.

1/4 cup (1/2 stick) unsalted (sweet) butter or margarine
1/4 cup vegetable oil
7 cups fresh corn off the cob (cut from about 17 8-inch cobs), or frozen corn kernels
1 cup very finely chopped onions
1/4 cup granulated sugar
2 teaspoons Chef Paul Prudhomme's Seafood Magic
2 1/4 cups chicken, beef, or pork stock
1/4 cup (1/2 stick) unsalted (sweet) margarine
1 cup evaporated milk
1 pound crawfish tails
2 large eggs

In a large skillet, combine the butter and oil with the corn, onions, sugar, and Seafood Magic. Cook over high heat until the corn is tender and starch starts to form a crust on the pan bottom, about 12 to 14 minutes, stirring occasionally, and stirring more as the mixture starts sticking to the skillet. Gradually stir in 1 cup of the stock, scraping the pan bottom to remove the crust as you stir. Continue cooking for 5 minutes, stirring occasionally. Add the margarine and stir until melted. Cook for about 5 minutes, stirring frequently, and scraping the pan bottom as needed. Reduce the heat to low and cook for about 10 minutes, stirring occasionally. Add 1/4 cup more of the stock and cook about 15 minutes, stirring fairly frequently. Add the remaining 1 cup of stock and cook for about 10 minutes, stirring occasionally. Stir in 1/2 cup of the milk and continue cooking for about 5 minutes, or until

(continued)

most of the liquid is absorbed, stirring occasionally. Add the crawfish tails and bring the mixture to a boil. Immediately remove the pan from the heat.

In a bowl, combine the eggs and the remaining 1/2 cup of milk. Beat the mixture with a metal whisk for about 1 minute, or until very frothy. Add to the corn, stirring well. Serve immediately, allowing about 1/2 cup per person.

Mushroom-Barley Vegetable Soup

Makes 10 to 12 servings

H ere is a favorite recipe of actress Estelle Harris. (She plays George Costanza's mother on "Seinfeld.") Estelle appeared on "Live" with Kathie Lee and the Smothers Brothers and told the viewers that she has been acting since she was born, but only during the last twenty-two years has she been paid for it. This soup is based on one Estelle's mother used to make that included mushrooms, barley, and lamb. After Estelle got married (more than forty years ago!), she wanted to improve the recipe and make it her own, so she added split peas and a lot of vegetables. Because her daughter, Taryn, and daughter-in-law, Caryl, are both vegetarians, she omitted the meat and further adapted the recipe to suit their preference. Estelle emphasized that you, too, can adjust this recipe to your personal taste. You can even add the meat or soup bones at the beginning of the recipe, if you want.

1 1/2 cups pearl barley
1/2 cup yellow and green split peas
1 package (3 1/2 ounces) dried mushrooms
4 celery stalks, chopped
3 large onions, peeled and chopped
3 large carrots, chopped
2 sweet potatoes, peeled and chopped
2 white potatoes, peeled and chopped
1 large tomato, peeled and chopped
1 large parsnip, chopped
2 to 4 cups of other vegetables of your choice such as
    zucchini, cauliflower, okra, or broccoli
1/4 bunch chopped fresh dill
1/4 bunch chopped fresh parsley
Salt and pepper to taste (optional)
1 pound fresh mushrooms, sliced

(continued)

Bring a large pot of water to a boil. Add the barley, split peas, and dried mushrooms. Reduce the heat and simmer for about 70 minutes. Add all the remaining ingredients except the fresh mushrooms and continue cooking for about 45 minutes longer, or until the vegetables are tender. About 10 minutes before you are ready to serve the soup, add the fresh mushrooms and finish cooking.

Regis and Kathie Lee have fun as the set fills up with smoke for the Halloween festivities.

Luciano's Roasted Red Pepper Appetizer

The Mona Lisa restaurant in Stamford, Connecticut, is a frequent stop of Regis's when he is at his weekend home. Chef Luciano Magliulo reports that the restaurant is always a lot more lively when Regis is there, stopping at tables and chatting with people. This friendly chef learned how to make this appetizer about 18 years ago in Italy. It's a favorite among the Mona Lisa's clients because they like the presentation and the roasted red peppers. Raisins add an intriguing touch of sweetness to the dish.

4 red bell peppers
1/4 pound mozzarella cheese, cut into 3-by-1/2-inch strips
2 tablespoons pine nuts
2 tablespoons raisins
2 tablespoons extra-virgin olive oil
Salt and freshly ground black pepper to taste

Preheat the broiler. Position a broiler pan so that the tops of the peppers will be about 2 inches from the heat source. Roast the peppers for about 15 minutes, turning about every 5 minutes, until the skins are blistered and charred. Transfer the peppers to a bowl, cover, and let steam until cooled.

Preheat the oven to 400°F.

Peel the skin from the peppers. Cut each pepper into 3 large pieces. Remove the seeds and ribs.

Divide the strips of cheese evenly among the pieces of pepper. Sprinkle the pine nuts and raisins evenly over the cheese strips. Roll each piece of pepper around the filling and secure each closed with a toothpick.

Place the rolled peppers in a baking pan. Drizzle with the olive oil and season with the salt and pepper. Bake for about 5 minutes, or until the cheese is melted.

Crystal's Bunzas

Makes 6 servings

Actress Crystal Carson, a native Nebraskan, appeared on "Live" with her modernized version of a bunza, an envelope of bread dough filled with a savory meat-and-cabbage mixture. Bunzas were first created in Nebraska by people of Russian-German descent, and now these hearty sandwiches are the main attraction at a chain of restaurants in Nebraska. Crystal says this is her mother's recipe and that she herself likes to eat bunzas after a hard day on the set of "General Hospital," where she plays the power-driven, ambitious entrepreneur, Julia Barrett. Crystal has also appeared on "Cheers" and "thirtysomething"; she starred in *Killer Tomatoes Strike Back* and appeared with Madonna in *Who's That Girl?*

The morning of the show, Crystal arrived at "Live" to find that the frozen bread dough had not been thawed and was still rock-solid. Knowing that the show must go on, she microwaved the dough, then put it in a low oven to try to get it to rise. Fortunately, she had rehearsed the recipe the night before and tucked one of the completed bunzas into her purse. This became the finished sample that Regis ate on the show. (We think Crystal would have made a great audience member for "Let's Make a Deal!")

Serve these sandwiches with a salad and french fries, or for a lower-calorie meal, serve bunzas with salad and broccoli. To make Italian-style bunzas, add a little spaghetti or pizza sauce to the filling mixture.

> 2 pounds of homemade bread dough or store-bought frozen dough that has been thawed according to the package directions (this is enough dough to make two 1-pound loaves of bread)
> 1 tablespoon butter or margarine (optional)
> Nonstick vegetable cooking spray

1 medium onion, chopped
6 mushrooms, sliced
1/4 cup water
1 small head cabbage, shredded
1 pound ground beef
Salt, pepper, and garlic powder to taste
6 slices of cheddar cheese

Let the thawed dough rise for 30 to 60 minutes at room temperature.

Meanwhile, in a saucepan, melt the butter over medium-high heat. Or spray the saucepan with nonstick vegetable cooking spray. Add the onion and mushrooms and cook for 5 to 10 minutes, or until the mushrooms are softened and the onion is translucent.

In a large saucepot, bring the water to a boil. Add the cabbage and cook for about 10 minutes, or until the cabbage is soft.

In a large skillet, cook the ground beef, salt, pepper, and garlic powder until the beef is browned. Drain the fat from the skillet and discard.

Add the beef and onion mixtures to the cabbage and stir together.

Preheat the oven to 350°F. and spray a baking sheet with nonstick vegetable cooking spray.

Cut the bread dough into 6 equal-size pieces. Spray a work surface with nonstick vegetable cooking spray and roll each piece of dough into an 8-inch square. Spoon one-sixth of the beef and cabbage mixture onto the center of each piece of dough. Place a piece of cheese on top of each square.

Pinch together the two opposite sides of each square. Seal the ends and tuck them under.

Place the "envelopes" on the prepared baking sheet, folded sides down, and bake for 25 to 30 minutes, or until golden brown.

(continued)

For a Reduced-calorie Version of Bunzas: Omit the butter and use the cooking spray. Use only 1/2 pound of ground beef and increase the cabbage to 1 large or 2 small heads of cabbage. Omit the cheese or use low-fat cheese.

For Smaller Bunzas: Divide the dough into 8 equal-size pieces. Roll each piece of dough into an 8-by-5-inch rectangle. Fill with one-eighth of the mixture. Fold in the 5-inch sides so that the edges of the dough meet, and pinch them together as best you can. Then fold in the 8-inch sides to cover the 5-inch sides. Bake with the folded sides down. Makes 8 individual smaller bunzas.

Old-Fashioned Vegetable Potpie

Makes 4 servings

For celebrating the harvest moon, there may be no better recipe than this potpie, chock-full of fall harvest vegetables. Chef Scott Cohen of Tatou, a premier supper club in New York City, demonstrated his recipe for an easy one-pot meal. This version uses fall vegetables, but it could also include cubes of cooked chicken, turkey, or beef, or the same amount of vegetables from other seasons.

Scott pointed out that the recipe for his piecrust is very easy to remember. It is called "3-2-1 pie dough" because it uses 3 cups of flour, 2 cups of vegetable shortening, and 1 cup of ice water. As a special salute to the moon, cut out half-moon-shaped slivers from the top of the pie, using the point of a sharp knife.

POTPIE FILLING

2 tablespoons olive oil
1 red onion, diced
1 yellow turnip, diced
1 large carrot, diced
1 zucchini, diced
1 yellow squash, diced
2 garlic cloves, finely chopped
Salt, pepper, ground cumin, and cayenne to taste
2 tomatoes, diced

DOUGH

3 cups all-purpose flour
2 cups hydrogenated vegetable shortening, cut into 1-inch
   pieces
Approximately 1 cup ice water mixed with a pinch of salt
1 egg, lightly beaten

(continued)

To Make the Potpie Filling: In a 10- to 12-inch cast iron skillet, heat the oil over medium-high heat. When the oil is hot, add the onion and cook for 5 to 10 minutes, or until the onion is translucent. Stir in the remaining ingredients except the tomatoes and cook for about 5 minutes. Add the tomatoes and simmer for 5 minutes more. Spoon the mixture into a bowl and refrigerate until it is cool. Wipe out the skillet.

To Make the Dough: In a large bowl, stir together the flour and shortening until the dough forms walnut-size balls. Mix in enough of the water gradually until the dough starts to pull together and forms a ball. Divide the dough in half and pat each piece of dough into a disk. Wrap each disk in waxed paper or plastic wrap and refrigerate for 5 minutes, or until the dough is firm enough to roll out.

Preheat the oven to 400°F. On a lightly floured work surface with a lightly floured rolling pin, roll out each piece of dough into a circle about 2 inches larger than the skillet.

Carefully transfer a circle of dough to the skillet and ease it into the pan. Brush the dough with some of the beaten egg.

Spoon the vegetables onto the dough in the skillet. Place the remaining circle of dough over the top. Turn the edges of the pie dough under and crimp them together. If you like, make cutouts in the top of the pie. Glaze the top of the pie with the beaten egg. Bake for 35 to 50 minutes, or until the crust is golden brown.

Tagliolini alla Ligure

Makes 4 servings

L e Madri restaurant, located in the Chelsea section of Manhattan, serves regional Italian cuisine. Chef Pino Luongo appeared on "Live" on Columbus Day and prepared this pasta dish, which is traditionally served in the Liguria region of Italy. (Christopher Columbus came from Genoa, which is Liguria's capital city.) The pesto, white beans, and *haricots verts* in this recipe are all representative of this region.

On "Live," Pino tried to teach Regis how to "flip" the pasta in the pan, but it all ended up being very messy and not especially successful. Next time, Rege! If you think flipping pasta in a large skillet is something better left to the pros, return the drained pasta to the large pot in which it was cooked. Add the sauce and Parmesan cheese to the pasta and toss gently with two wooden spoons.

Pino recommends serving his flavorful pasta recipe with a good crusty bread and a fresh fruit tart as a delightful lunch. Accompany this recipe with a simple fish roasted with lemon and herbs and you have created dinner. Accompany it with a light, slightly fruity wine, such as a Vermentino from Liguria, and you'll wonder why Columbus ever left home.

PESTO SAUCE
1 large bunch of basil, stems removed
1/2 cup pine nuts
2 garlic cloves, peeled
4 to 6 tablespoons olive oil
Salt and pepper to taste

PASTA
3/4 cup *haricots verts* (thin French string beans) or green beans
1 pound fresh tagliolini pasta (or 1 pound of fettuccine)
1/2 cup extra-virgin olive oil

(continued)

3/4 cup cooked cannellini beans
Freshly grated Parmesan cheese to taste

To Make the Pesto Sauce: In the container of a food processor fitted with the metal chopping blade or in a blender, process the basil, pine nuts, garlic, and 3 tablespoons of the olive oil. Gradually add more olive oil until the pesto has the consistency of a thick, rich paste. Season with salt and pepper.

To Make the Pasta: Submerge the haricots verts in boiling water for about 1 minute. Drain.

Bring a large pot of salted water to a boil. Add the pasta and cook just until *al dente.*

Meanwhile, in a large skillet, heat the olive oil over low heat. Add the cannellini beans, haricots verts, and pesto and stir to let the flavors blend.

Drain a small amount of the pasta water into the skillet to thin the sauce slightly. Drain the pasta completely. Add the pasta to the sauce and mix it by flipping the pasta in the pan until the sauce has blended thoroughly with the pasta. Sprinkle the Parmesan cheese over the pasta and sauce mixture and toss again. Serve immediately.

Time-saving Tips: While fresh is best, you can also use canned cannellini beans that have been rinsed and drained, and use a high-quality store-bought brand of pesto sauce.

Tips for Relaxed Entertaining with Pino Luongo

~~❡~~

*P*ino reports, "I don't do formal entertaining. When you come to my home, you are greeted with a glass of wine and we all go to the kitchen. I believe entertaining is best when it's a team effort.

"The great thing about the preceding recipe is that there is something for everyone to help with. Someone can clean the haricots verts, someone else can clean the basil and pull off the leaves, then a team of guests can make the pesto, and then everything gets tossed together. The whole process would take about 15 minutes. With everyone helping, conversation flows in a relaxed, easy way. Everyone is involved, but no one has to help if they don't want to. I don't like people to wait, open-mouthed, to be fed. I like them to feel relaxed, like they are at home.

"My other house rule is no hard liquor before dinner. Great food should be complemented with great wine only!"

*C*azzuola

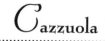

Makes 4 servings

Chef Gianfranco (Gianni) Audieri of the San Francisco restaurant Fior d'Italia appeared on "Live" to demonstrate this recipe from the Lombardy region of northern Italy. *Cazzuola* is especially popular in Milan, Lombardy's capital. Fior d'Italia is the oldest Italian restaurant in America. Appropriately, Gianni selected this recipe because all the ingredients have been in existence since before Christopher Columbus discovered the Americas.

(continued)

1 pound fresh bacon (pork underbelly), in one piece
1 pound baby back ribs
1 pound sweet Italian sausage
1 tablespoon olive oil
1 large onion, diced
1 celery heart, diced
1 large carrot, diced
1 large green cabbage, shredded
1/4 cup red wine vinegar
Salt and pepper to taste

Place the fresh bacon and 3 cups of water in a large saucepot. Bring the water to a boil and boil for 1 hour. Add more water, if necessary, to keep the bacon covered.

Meanwhile, in a large skillet, sear the ribs and sausage over medium-high heat, turning occasionally, until well browned.

Preheat the oven to 425°F.

In a Dutch oven or large heavy ovenproof saucepot, heat the oil over medium-high heat. Cook the onion, celery, and carrot for 7 to 10 minutes, or until the vegetables are softened. Add the cabbage and vinegar and cook for about 10 minutes more. Place the cooked fresh bacon, ribs, and sausage in the saucepot. Pour the water from boiling the fresh bacon into the saucepot. Season with salt and pepper. Cover and bake in the oven for about 1 hour. Slice the meats and arrange with the vegetables on a serving dish.

$\mathcal{A}$utumn $\mathcal{P}$ork $\mathcal{C}$hops

Makes 4 servings

Francis Anthony, the Love Chef, frequently appears on "Live with Regis & Kathie Lee." For more of his recipes, check out his books, *Cooking with Love* and *Cooking with Love Italian Style.*

> 1 tablespoon celery seeds
> 1 teaspoon ground coriander
> 4 center pork loin chops, trimmed of visible fat
> 1 tablespoon butter
> 1 small tart apple, cored and thinly sliced
> 1 small onion, thinly sliced
> 1 tablespoon firmly packed brown sugar
> 1 tablespoon water
> Salt, if desired
> Freshly ground pepper to taste

Sprinkle the celery seeds and coriander on waxed paper. Press each side of the chops into the mixture until they are evenly coated.

In a large skillet, heat the butter over medium heat until it is melted. Add the pork chops, apple slices, onion, sugar, and water. Season with salt and pepper.

Cover the skillet. Reduce the heat to low and cook the chops for 10 to 15 minutes on each side, or until the chops are cooked the way you like them.

European-style Pot Roast

Makes 8 to 10 servings

 A native of Germany, Chef Tell always adds an innovative flair to even basic dishes such as pot roast.

2 tablespoons olive oil
1 (4- to 5-pound) eye round roast
2 tablespoons tomato paste
2 garlic cloves, finely chopped
4 cups beef stock or broth
2 cups red wine
2 bay leaves
7 tablespoons lightly salted butter, divided
6 medium carrots, diced
6 medium celery stalks, diced
2 medium onions, diced
6 tablespoons all-purpose flour
Salt and pepper to taste

In a Dutch oven or a large, heavy saucepot, heat the oil over medium-high heat. Add the meat and brown on all sides. Add the tomato paste and garlic and cook until the garlic is lightly browned. Add the beef stock, wine, and bay leaves. Over high heat, bring the mixture to a boil. Reduce the heat to low, cover the pan tightly, and simmer (do not boil) for about 2 hours.

While the meat is cooking, in a large skillet, heat 1 tablespoon of the butter over medium-high heat. Add the carrots, celery, and onions and cook for 5 to 10 minutes, or until softened slightly. Add the vegetable mixture to the Dutch oven after the meat has cooked for 2 hours. Cover and continue cooking 30 to 60 minutes longer, or until the meat is tender.

Transfer the meat and vegetables to a serving platter. Pour the cooking liquid into a large bowl and reserve. Discard the bay leaves.

In the Dutch oven over medium heat, melt the remaining 6 tablespoons of butter. Whisk or stir in the flour until smooth and bubbly. Continue cooking, stirring constantly, for 2 to 3 minutes. Gradually whisk in the reserved beef stock, blending completely after each addition. Cook, stirring constantly, until the mixture boils and thickens. Season the sauce with salt and pepper.

Slice the roast and serve with the vegetables and the sauce.

All dressed up for Halloween, Kathie Lee gives Regis a playful kiss on the cheek.

Sylvia's World-Famous Barbecued Ribs

For soul food, the place to go is Sylvia's Restaurant in Harlem. Chef/owner Sylvia Woods appeared on "Live" and demonstrated her one-of-a-kind recipe for ribs and sauce that she brought to the Big Apple from South Carolina. She has been making these ribs for thirty years and learned the recipe from her grandmother.

Sylvia's recipe makes a generous quantity of sauce, so you will have some to use at another time. "It's very hard to cook bad ribs as long as you've got good sauce," she says. She recommends always keeping a jar of this sauce in the refrigerator. Adjust the amount of sugar and hot pepper sauce to your taste. The Southern way to prepare ribs is to cook them without barbecue sauce so that they get crispy, and to serve the sauce on the side. For moist ribs, slather the ribs with the sauce after you remove them from the vinegar and before they are baked the final 20 to 30 minutes.

Throughout her segment, Sylvia kept referring to the host as "Regin." "Regin" (who is notorious himself for messing up people's names) thought it was pretty funny and announced, "Regin at your service!"

On "Live," Sylvia served the ribs with corn bread, collard greens, and yams—all great suggestions as foods to serve at your own soul-food meal.

RIBS

1 tablespoon salt
1 tablespoon ground black pepper
3 1/2 pounds pork ribs
1 tablespoon crushed red pepper flakes
2 cups distilled white vinegar

BARBECUE SAUCE

2 cups tomato purée

2 cups water

2 cups granulated sugar

1 cup hot pepper sauce (Sylvia recommends Louisiana Hot Sauce)

1 celery stalk, finely chopped

1 green pepper, seeded and finely chopped

1/2 medium onion, finely chopped

1 tablespoon crushed red pepper flakes

2 large lemons

To Make the Ribs: Preheat the oven to 375°F. In a small bowl, stir together the salt and pepper. Sprinkle the mixture over the ribs and "lovingly" rub it into them. Do the same with the crushed red pepper flakes.

Pour the vinegar into a glass dish that is large enough to hold the ribs. Add the ribs and bake for 60 to 90 minutes. (Test the meat after 60 minutes. You don't want it to be falling off the bones.) Reduce the oven temperature to 350°F.

Discard the vinegar mixture and transfer the ribs to a baking pan. Bake for 20 to 30 minutes longer.

Meanwhile, to Make the Barbecue Sauce: In a large saucepan, stir together the tomato purée, water, sugar, hot pepper sauce, celery, green pepper, onion, and crushed red pepper flakes. Squeeze the lemons over the pan, discarding any seeds. Cut the lemons into 1/4-inch-thick slices and add them to the pot. Simmer the mixture (do not let it boil or it will become too thin) for 30 minutes.

Serve the ribs with the sauce. Discard the lemon slices, cover, and refrigerate any leftover sauce for another use.

Perfect Beef Stew

When there's a nip in the air and a full harvest moon, it's always nice to warm yourself with a hearty meal. This deluxe version of beef stew from Chef Tell is just the right solution when you are looking for a really satisfying meal. To julienne means to cut the food into matchstick-size pieces.

6 tablespoons vegetable oil
2 pounds boneless beef, cut into 1 1/2-inch cubes
Salt and pepper to taste
2 potatoes, peeled and diced
1 cup julienned carrots
1 cup julienned leeks
1 cup julienned celery
1 onion, peeled and sliced
3 cups beef or chicken stock
1/2 cup red wine
1 bay leaf
12 ounces noodles, cooked according to package directions

In a large saucepot, heat the oil over medium-high heat. Add the beef cubes and cook until browned on all sides. Season with the salt and pepper.

Add the potatoes, carrots, leeks, celery, and onion and cook for 5 minutes, or until the vegetables are softened slightly.

Add the stock, wine, and bay leaf and simmer, covered, for 30 to 35 minutes, or until the meat is tender. Remove the bay leaf.

Add the cooked noodles to the pot and gently toss to combine.

Baked Apple Dumplings

Makes 4 servings

Squares of puff pastry are wrapped around apples in this charming recipe from Chef Tell. Melted vanilla ice cream forms an easy creamy sauce to accompany this old-fashioned dessert.

4 6-inch squares of puff pastry dough
4 tablespoons granulated sugar
4 tablespoons raisins
4 medium apples, peeled and cored
2 eggs, lightly beaten
1 pint of vanilla ice cream

Preheat the oven to 375°F.

Using a floured rolling pin, on a lightly floured work surface, roll out a square of the puff pastry so that it is large enough to wrap around 1 of the apples.

Sprinkle the center of the puff pastry square with 1 tablespoon of the sugar. Place 1 tablespoon of the raisins in the center of the pastry. Place an apple on top of the raisins. Brush some of the beaten eggs over the surrounding dough. Bring up all the sides so that the apple is covered and press the sides together at the top. Place the covered apple upside down on a baking sheet. Brush the outside of the dumpling with the egg mixture. Repeat the procedure with the remaining puff pastry squares, sugar, raisins, and apples. Bake the dumplings for 20 to 30 minutes, or until the pastry is lightly browned.

Melt the ice cream to create a sauce. Serve the baked apple dumplings on top of pools of the sauce.

Chapter 12

Let's All Give Thanks

·············~❦~·············

When it comes to getting together with friends and family to eat, there is probably no holiday more universally celebrated in the United States than Thanksgiving. At this time of the year we reflect on our heritage as Americans, and celebrate the bounty of the harvest by stuffing ourselves with delicious foods!

The following chapter contains recipes for some delightful traditional foods, such as Chef Al Hynes's New England Clam Chowder, a one-hundred-year-old recipe. Al's appearance on "Live" marked the first time he had ever shared this family treasure. Of course we've included a recipe for turkey and an out-of-the-ordinary one it is, too. However, Thompson's Turkey as demonstrated by Vogue magazine's food editor, Jeffrey Steingarten, could well become a tradition in your home. For dessert, two "Live" regulars,

Chef Tell and the Love Chef, created, respectively, recipes for Pumpkin Pie and Pumpkin Cheesecake.

As you page through this chapter and plan your next Thanksgiving celebration, get ready to loosen up your belt buckles.

Tips for Thanksgiving

~❦~

- Make piecrusts up to three weeks ahead of time and freeze.

- When you find yourself with stale bread on hand in the weeks preceding Thanksgiving, cut it into cubes for use in stuffing. Freeze the bread cubes in plastic bags until you need them.

- Make your holiday less stressful by reintroducing the "progressive dinner." For less work and more variety, have appetizers at one home, the main course at another, and dessert at a third.

- If you are entertaining any serious sports fans, plan to serve the meal at a time that won't conflict with televised football games.

- Plan well ahead which glasses, cutlery, and china you will be using, and have them washed, shined, and ready. Decide in advance on the serving dishes, too, and label each one with a stick-on note reminding you of its purpose.

- Carve out the centers of artichokes and insert votive candles in them. Arrange them among pumpkins, squash, and gourds for a natural-looking centerpiece. Pineapples, a symbol of welcome, also can serve as candleholders if you remove some of the center leaves.

- Cut out holes in the centers of miniature pumpkins and use them as festive candleholders. Or completely scrape out the insides of small pumpkins and fill them with cranberry relish.

- Create a centerpiece with edible take-home treats. For instance, fill a pretty basket with decorated jars of jams and jellies and wrapped loaves of quick bread.

- Spray gold paint on nuts, leaves, and lady apples. Add streamers of gold floral ribbon to make a seasonal table setting. Or spray small baskets or a cornucopia with gold paint and fill them with the season's bounty. To complete the look, serve dessert chocolates or scoops of Italian ice on larger gilded leaves.

- Create napkin rings out of breadstick dough. Tie into shapes and bake at a low temperature until hard, then varnish with clear shellac.

- Plan activities for children at your Thanksgiving get-togethers. Put together "activity bags" ahead of time.

- Another idea is to have the makings for graham-cracker houses and let each child make one (as Joy demonstrated on "Live"). Give the children and the young-at-heart graham crackers, frosting, and an assortment of candies and let the building begin!

- On the day itself, save some preparation tasks for helpful guests who want to join you in the kitchen.

- As an alternative to appetite-killing hors d'oeuvres, pass the first course on small plates before the guests are seated.

- A specialty coffee bar ends the day with a flourish. Serve Irish Coffee, Kahlua Coffee, and the like for drinkers; offer Cardamom Coffee with a cracked cardamom pod per cup or Viennese Coffee with sweetened whipped cream and a dusting of cinnamon for nondrinkers.

How do you celebrate Thanksgiving?

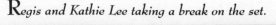

Regis: It's turkey every year. My favorite stuffing, which I argue with Kathie Lee about, has raisins in it. We always do it at home and have some friends over. Joy makes a big vegetable and fruit centerpiece with walnuts and leaves. We ask the girls what they are thankful for, and they respond. We agree that it's important for a family to count their blessings, at least once a year. People really should do that because there is a lot to be thankful for in this country.

Kathie Lee: We usually spend Thanksgiving at my parents' home. My mother's Thanksgiving is my favorite meal of the year. I love her turkey, stuffing, mashers, and candied sweet potatoes. If I could eat the same thing every night, it would be that—of course I'd weigh eight hundred pounds! Her Thanksgiving dinner goes on all day long. When we have a turkey, we all start eating it as soon as it comes out of the oven. My mother makes twice as much gravy as she would ordinarily need because she knows that we will all start tearing off pieces of meat and dipping it into the gravy.

Regis and Kathie Lee taking a break on the set.

Suzy's Squash Soup

Makes 6 to 8 servings

Assistant producer Suzy Hayman-DeYoung created this recipe with her husband for his parents' anniversary. Since then, it has become a favorite that they serve again and again. When Suzy entertains she likes to play classical music in the background—quietly, so that guests can converse easily.

4 acorn squash
About 3 tablespoons unsalted (sweet) butter
About 3 tablespoons honey
2 medium to large sweet potatoes
2 cups chicken broth
2 cups milk
A couple of pinches of freshly grated nutmeg
1/2 cup heavy (whipping) cream
1/2 cup medium-dry sherry
Salt and pepper to taste
Chopped fresh parsley, for garnish

Preheat the oven to 350°F.

Cut each squash in half across the width and scrape out the seeds. Place the squash halves on a jelly-roll pan or baking sheet. Add a little butter and honey to the center of each half. Cover the squash with aluminum foil to prevent them from burning or drying out. Bake for 1 hour, or until the squash are tender when pierced with the tines of a fork.

Meanwhile, peel the sweet potatoes and cut them into thick slices. Cook in boiling water for 20 to 30 minutes, or until they are tender. Drain.

Scoop out the flesh from the tender squash into a 4-quart saucepot. Add the sweet potatoes and the chicken broth. Place the pot over low heat and add the milk and the nutmeg. Simmer for 20 to 30 minutes, crushing the pieces of squash and sweet potato with a wooden spoon against the side of the pot.

(continued)

Let the soup cool slightly. In the container of a blender or a food processor fitted with the metal chopping blade, process the soup mixture in batches until smooth. Return the soup to the pot. Stir in the heavy cream and the sherry and bring the soup back to a simmer. Season with salt and pepper. If the soup is too thick, add a little more broth, milk, or cream. Sprinkle the top of the soup with parsley and serve.

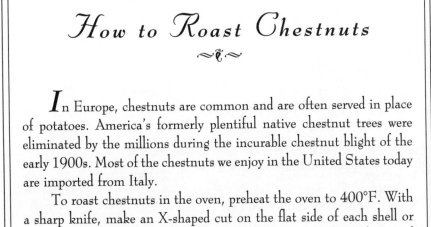

How to Roast Chestnuts

In Europe, chestnuts are common and are often served in place of potatoes. America's formerly plentiful native chestnut trees were eliminated by the millions during the incurable chestnut blight of the early 1900s. Most of the chestnuts we enjoy in the United States today are imported from Italy.

To roast chestnuts in the oven, preheat the oven to 400°F. With a sharp knife, make an X-shaped cut on the flat side of each shell or prick each shell with the tines of a fork. Place on a baking sheet and bake for 10 to 15 minutes. When the chestnuts are just cool enough to handle, shell them and remove the inner brown skins. (Using a dish towel helps.)

If you really want to get into the spirit of the season and "roast them on an open fire," position the chestnuts at the edge of the fire near the glowing coals. Let them roast for about 10 minutes, turning frequently, until you hear them "pop." Remove them from the coals, let cool slightly, then remove the shells. (The dish towel is really valuable here as there is often ash on the chestnuts.)

New England Clam Chowder

Makes 8 servings

Al Hynes's appearance on "Live" was the first time he had ever shared the recipe for his popular and famous clam chowder. It is a hundred-year-old family recipe that he has been serving for twenty-five years at Thompson's Clam Bar Restaurant in Harwichport, Massachusetts. Each week, restaurant patrons consume six hundred and fifty gallons of Al's hearty chowder. While he makes it in batches of sixty gallons, the following version has been scaled down to serve eight.

1/2 cup (1 stick) unsalted (sweet) butter
1 cup chopped Spanish onion
1 cup chopped celery
1/2 cup all-purpose flour
4 bottles (8 ounces each) clam juice, heated
12 ounces chopped fresh or frozen clams
2 1/2 ounces scored salt pork or fatback
2 fish or clam bouillon cubes
2 cups diced potatoes
2 cups half-and-half, heated

In a large saucepot over medium-high heat, melt the butter. Stir in the onion and celery and cook for 5 to 7 minutes, or until the vegetables are translucent. Stir in the flour and cook for about 5 minutes, stirring constantly. Gradually stir in the heated clam juice.

Add the clams, salt pork, and bouillon cubes and cook for 20 minutes.

Meanwhile, cook the potatoes for about 15 minutes in boiling water. Using a slotted spoon, transfer the potatoes to the clam juice mixture and let stand for 20 minutes. Remove the salt pork and stir in the heated half-and-half.

Roasted Chestnut Bisque

This soup recipe from Francis Anthony, the Love Chef, would make an excellent start to your Thanksgiving feasting. Or after the major celebration is over, you could serve a cup of this soup along with leftover turkey sandwiches.

1 pound leeks (about 3)
2 tablespoons unsalted (sweet) butter
2 1/2 cups strong turkey or chicken stock or broth
1 pound freshly roasted chestnuts (see box on page 234), shelled
1 small carrot, chopped
3/4 cup light cream
1/2 cup Marsala
1/2 teaspoon ground white pepper
1/4 teaspoon freshly grated nutmeg
1/2 cup sour cream

Cut off the roots and tough green tops of the leeks. Peel away the coarse outer layers of each leek, split down to the root end, and wash the inner leaves thoroughly to remove any grit. Chop the leeks into 1/2-inch pieces.

In a large saucepan, heat the butter over medium-high heat. Add the leeks and cook for 6 to 8 minutes, or until they are softened but not browned. Add the stock, chestnuts, and carrot and simmer for about 18 minutes, or until the chestnuts and carrot are tender.

In the container of a blender or a food processor fitted with the metal chopping blade, process the soup until smooth. Return the mixture to the pan and stir in the cream, Marsala, pepper, and nutmeg. Bring to a simmer over low heat. Serve in warmed soup bowls topped with a dollop of sour cream.

Turkey Marsala

Makes 4 servings

H ere's an elegant way to serve turkey without having to deal with the whole bird. If you are having a small get-together for Thanksgiving, this recipe from the Love Chef is one you might want to try. It would be lovely with a wild rice dish.

4 turkey breast cutlets
All-purpose flour for dredging the turkey
2 tablespoons unsalted (sweet) butter
1 tablespoon olive oil
1 cup plus 1 tablespoon Marsala, divided
4 large shallots, sliced
1 cup chicken stock or broth
1 cup fresh mushrooms, sliced
1/4 teaspoon dried sage leaves
Salt and freshly ground black pepper to taste
Chopped fresh parsley, for garnish
1 lemon, cut into thin slices, for garnish

D ip the turkey cutlets in the flour to lightly coat both sides; shake off any excess.

I n a large skillet, heat the butter and oil over medium heat. Add 1 tablespoon of the Marsala. Cook the turkey cutlets for about 3 to 5 minutes on each side, or until lightly browned. Transfer the cutlets to a warm plate.

A dd the shallots to the pan and cook for 4 to 6 minutes, or until they are transparent. Add the remaining 1 cup of Marsala, scraping up the browned bits from the bottom of the skillet. Add the chicken stock and simmer for 8 to 10 minutes, or until the sauce is reduced by about half. Add the mushrooms and sage and cook for about 5 minutes. Return the turkey to the skillet and heat through. Season with salt and pepper. Transfer the turkey to a serving platter. Garnish with parsley and lemon slices.

$\mathcal{V}ogue's\ \mathcal{V}ersion\ of$
$\mathcal{T}hompson's\ \mathcal{T}urkey$

Makes 1 or more servings (see quote from Robert Benchley below)

orton Thompson was an esteemed journalist and author of the 1930s and 1940s who occasionally wrote about food. In the mid-1930s, he published an elaborate recipe for turkey that has been printed many times in the popular press. In the November 1992 issue of *Vogue*, Jeffrey Steingarten, the magazine's food critic, wrote about his trials and tribulations while preparing a Thompson Turkey. His article and the accompanying photograph of this "blackened turkey" so intrigued the producers of "Live" that they broke their rule of featuring only simple recipes and asked Jeffrey to prepare his version of the notable Thompson Turkey on the show.

Here's a little history on this elusive bird. Jeffrey's wife's family first introduced him to the Thompson Turkey by showing him a tattered article by Robert Benchley in a 1957 issue of *Gourmet*. It read, in part:

> Several years ago, I ate a turkey prepared and roasted by Morton Thompson. I didn't eat the whole turkey, but that wasn't my fault. There were outsiders present who ganged up on me. . . . I will just say that I decided at that time that Morton Thompson was the greatest man since [Brillat-] Savarin, and for all I know, Savarin wasn't as good as Morton Thompson.

Jeffrey reports that this is basically how you make a Thompson's Turkey:

> You first mix up Thompson's elaborate stuffing, sew it tight into a very large turkey, and brown the bird briefly at a very high temperature. Then you paint it with a paste of flour,

egg, and onion juice, dry it in the oven, and paint it again, repeating this until the bird is hermetically sealed under a stiff crust. You slowly roast the turkey for five hours, basting it every fifteen minutes. The bird emerges from the oven with a dead black surface from wing to wing.

You may wonder why anyone would want to do all this. In his fascinating *Vogue* article, Jeffrey let Morton Thompson explain:

Beneath this burnt, harmless, now worthless shell the bird will be golden and dark brown, succulent, giddy-making with wild aromas, crisp and crunchable and crackling. The meat beneath this crazing panorama of lip-wetting skin will be wet, juice will spurt from it in tiny fountains high as the handle of the fork plunged into it; the meat will be white, crammed with mocking flavor, delirious with things that rush over your palate and are drowned and gone as fast as you can swallow; cut a little of it with a spoon, it will spread on bread as eagerly and readily as soft wurst.

You do not have to be a carver to eat this turkey; speak harshly to it and it will fall apart.

This is the end of it. All but the dressing. No pen, unless it were filled with Thompson's gravy, can describe Thompson's dressing, and there is not paper enough in the world to contain the thoughts and adjectives it would set down, and not marble enough to serve for its monuments.

Here is Jeffrey's recipe for this "giddy-making" bird. If you get a chance, read his entertaining article (he received a James Beard award for food journalism). It takes a while to assemble the stuffing ingredients, so plan accordingly.

TURKEY AND RENDERED TURKEY FAT
1 turkey (16 to 22 pounds) plus giblets
1/2 cup water

BASTING LIQUID
Giblets
5 cups of water, divided

(continued)

1 bay leaf

1 garlic clove, peeled

1 teaspoon paprika

1/2 teaspoon ground coriander

Salt to taste

3 cups apple cider

STUFFING MIXTURE BOWL #1

1 can (20 ounces) crushed pineapple

1 can (10 ounces) water chestnuts, drained and coarsely
chopped

1 apple, peeled, cored, and diced

1 orange, peeled and diced

3 tablespoons chopped preserved ginger

Grated peel of 1/2 lemon

STUFFING MIXTURE BOWL #2

6 celery stalks, chopped medium-fine

4 large onions, chopped medium-fine

1/4 cup chopped fresh parsley

2 tablespoons chopped fresh oregano leaves

4 to 5 garlic cloves, finely chopped

1 tablespoon celery seeds

1 tablespoon chopped fresh thyme leaves

1 tablespoon chopped fresh sage leaves

2 teaspoons Colman's dry mustard

2 teaspoons caraway seeds

2 teaspoons poppy seeds

1 1/2 teaspoons finely chopped fresh marjoram leaves

1 1/2 teaspoons finely chopped fresh summer savory leaves

1 bay leaf, finely crushed

1 teaspoon ground black pepper

1 teaspoon salt

1/2 teaspoon ground mace

1/2 teaspoon turmeric

4 cloves, heads removed and finely chopped

STUFFING MIXTURE BOWL #3

1 1/2 pounds fresh bread crumbs

3/4 pound ground veal

1/4 pound ground pork
1/2 cup (1 stick) unsalted (sweet) butter, softened
The rendered turkey fat

TURKEY PREPARATION
Vegetable oil for rubbing on the turkey
Salt and pepper to taste

PASTE
4 large egg yolks
2 teaspoons Colman's dry mustard
2 garlic cloves, finely chopped
2 tablespoons of onion juice (run an onion through your food
   processor and catch the juice)
2 teaspoons lemon juice
1 teaspoon salt
4 pinches cayenne pepper
Sifted all-purpose flour

To Prepare the Rendered Turkey Fat: Remove all the loose fat from the inside of the turkey and chop it finely. Place the chopped fat in a saucepan with 1/2 cup of water. Bring the mixture to a boil, reduce the heat, and simmer until all the water has evaporated and you are left with clear fat and pieces of solids. Reserve the fat for use in the stuffing.

About 1 hour before you are ready to cook the turkey, preheat the oven to its highest temperature so that it is red hot. Wrap a roasting rack with heavily greased aluminum foil and place the rack in a roasting pan that is large enough to hold the turkey.

To Prepare the Basting Liquid: Chop the gizzard. In a large saucepan, combine 4 cups of the water, the gizzard, neck, heart, bay leaf, garlic, paprika, coriander, and salt to taste. Let this simmer while you prepare the dressing. Just before you are ready to use the basting liquid, stir in the cider and the remaining 1 cup of water until combined. Don't let it cook any longer, but keep it warm on top of the oven.

To Prepare the Stuffing: Mix in each bowl the contents of each bowl. When each bowl is well mixed, mix the 3 of them together. And

(continued)

241 / *Let's All Give Thanks*

mix it well. Mix it with your hands. Mix it until your forearms and wrists ache. Then mix it some more. Now toss it enough so that it isn't any longer a doughy mass.

To Prepare the Turkey: Brush the turkey's skin with the oil. Rub the bird inside and out with salt and pepper. (Make sure you keep the turkey refrigerated until you are ready to stuff it.)

Stuff your turkey, but not too fully. Pretty full, though. Stuff the neck. Sew up the bird and sew the wings to the turkey's body.

Place the turkey on the prepared rack, breast side down. Bake it in the red-hot oven for 15 minutes. Carefully turn the bird onto its back and bake 15 minutes longer. Turn your oven down to 325°F. Now, while the turkey is sizzling hot, paint it completely all over with the paste. Put it back in the oven. The paste will have set in a few minutes. Drag it out again. Paint every nook and cranny of it once more. Put it back in the oven. Keep doing this until you haven't any more paste left. Baste the turkey every 15 minutes with the basting liquid (12 to 15 times). After you have turned the oven down to 325°F., bake the turkey for 4 1/2 to 5 hours (depending on the size of the turkey), or until an instant-read thermometer reads about 180 to 185°F. in the thigh between the leg and the body, 170°F. in the breast, and 160°F. in the stuffing.

When you remove the turkey, it will be dead black. You will think, "My God! I have ruined it." Be calm. Take a tweezers and pry loose the paste coating. It will come off readily. Beneath this burnt, harmless, now worthless shell the bird will be golden and dark brown, succulent, giddy-making with wild aromas, crisp and crunchable and crackling. . . .

Gelman's Real American Stuffing

Makes enough stuffing to stuff a 14-pound turkey or goose, 2 ducks, or 6 to 7 Cornish hens

"**L**ive"'s Executive Producer Michael Gelman likes to include this recipe as part of his "country Thanksgiving" meal. Because he has a country home on Long Island and is a big fan of duckling, he often uses Long Island ducklings. Michael says that you can eliminate the stuffing and cut down on the amount of chicken broth you use to create a delicious wild rice side dish to serve at any time of year.

3 1/2 cups chicken broth, divided
3/4 cup wild rice, rinsed
1/4 cup (1/2 stick) unsalted (sweet) butter
2 cups wild mushrooms such as shiitake or oyster
   mushrooms
2 cups sliced celery
1 large onion, chopped
1/2 cup toasted walnuts
1/4 cup chopped dried fruit such as apricots or prunes
1 tablespoon poultry seasoning
4 cups dried cornbread stuffing
Salt and freshly ground black pepper to taste

Bring 2 1/4 cups of the chicken broth to a boil. Add the wild rice. Reduce the heat, cover, and simmer for about 50 minutes, or until the rice is just tender.

In a large saucepan, heat the butter over medium-high heat. When the butter is melted, add the mushrooms, celery, onion, and walnuts. Cook, stirring occasionally, for about 10 minutes, or until the vegetables are softened. Stir in the dried fruit and poultry seasoning. Remove the pan from the heat.

In a large bowl, mix together the rice mixture, the vegetable mixture, and the stuffing until combined. Add enough of the remaining 1 1/4 cups of chicken broth until the mixture is moist enough so that it sticks together. Use the mixture to stuff the poultry of your choice.

Fresh Cranberry-Citrus Relish

Makes 6 to 8 servings

As another part of Michael Gelman's country Thanksgiving, he likes to make this tart and refreshing relish. Good with turkey, it provides an especially effective counterpoint to heavier birds such as goose and duck. Stored, covered, in the refrigerator, the relish keeps for at least a week. Use it as an intriguing spread on turkey sandwiches.

1 package (12 ounces) fresh cranberries
1 cup firmly packed brown sugar
1/2 cup freshly squeezed orange juice
1 whole orange, peeled
1/4 cup maple syrup
1 tablespoon grated orange peel
1/2 teaspoon grated lemon peel
1/2 teaspoon ground cinnamon
1/2 teaspoon ground ginger
1/2 teaspoon ground cloves

Place all the ingredients in the container of a food processor fitted with the metal chopping blade. Process until the mixture is chopped to the consistency you like. Cover and refrigerate.

Delores's Delightful Candied Yams

Makes 4 servings

Segment producer Delores Spruell-Jackson enjoys this recipe from her grandmother every Thanksgiving. Every couple of years Delores goes to family reunions, usually in North Carolina, of about 150 people. This past year, Delores was in charge of coordinating the event in New York City, where they had the reunion at Sylvia's (see page 224), which serves Southern-style food. At Delores's family get-togethers a family talent show is always a part of their banquet dinner. There are talented musicians as well as poets within her family—some are famous and some are well-kept secrets. We think this is an idea you may want to include at your own party.

    1 pound sweet potatoes
    1 can (20 ounces) crushed pineapple, drained
    3/4 cup maple syrup
    3/4 cup brown sugar
    2 tablespoons unsalted (sweet) butter, cut into 1/2-inch
        pieces
    1 tablespoon vanilla extract
    Pinch of grated nutmeg
    Pinch of ground cinnamon

Peel the potatoes. Cook the potatoes in a large pot of boiling water until tender.

Preheat the oven to 350°F.

Cut the potatoes in half and place them in a 1 1/2-quart baking dish. Add the pineapple, maple syrup, brown sugar, butter, and vanilla. Sprinkle the top with the nutmeg and cinnamon. Bake for about 30 minutes, or until heated through.

$\mathcal{P}$umpkin $\mathcal{C}$heesecake

Cool and creamy Pumpkin Cheesecake could be just the thing to offer at your next Thanksgiving or holiday party. The Love Chef created this sublime dessert that is sure to get rave reviews from all who taste it.

7 egg whites plus 2 egg yolks, at room temperature
1 1/2 pounds (about 2 1/3 cups) ricotta cheese
1 cup granulated sugar
1 1/2 cups puréed cooked or canned pumpkin
1 1/2 tablespoons vanilla extract
1 teaspoon pumpkin-pie spice
1 teaspoon baking powder
Confectioners' sugar for sprinkling on top of the cheesecake

Preheat the oven to 350°F. Butter an 8-inch springform pan. Dust with flour and tap out the excess.

In a grease-free bowl, using an electric mixer, beat the egg whites until they form stiff, shiny peaks.

In another bowl, using the same beaters, beat the egg yolks, ricotta cheese, sugar, pumpkin, vanilla, pumpkin-pie spice, and baking powder, just until smooth. Using a rubber spatula, fold in the egg whites, just until combined. Scrape the batter into the prepared pan.

Bake for 75 to 85 minutes, or until a cake tester or toothpick inserted in the center comes out clean. Transfer the cheesecake to a wire rack and cool completely. Cover the cheesecake with plastic wrap and refrigerate for at least 6 hours, or until cold.

To serve, loosen the cake from the side of the pan by running a thin-bladed knife around the edge. Release the springform to remove the side of the pan. Slice the cake with a knife dipped in hot water and wiped dry. Dust the top of the cake with confectioners' sugar.

Chef Tell's Pumpkin Pie

Makes 8 servings

If you want to make a pumpkin pie from scratch, see Chef Tell's directions below on how to prepare fresh pumpkin. For extra holiday appeal, put sweetened whipped cream in a pastry bag fitted with a star tip and pipe rosettes on the pie.

2 cups canned or cooked fresh pumpkin
1 1/2 cups heavy (whipping) cream
3 large eggs, lightly beaten
1/2 cup granulated sugar
1/4 cup firmly packed brown sugar
1 tablespoon ground cinnamon
1/2 teaspoon salt
1/4 teaspoon grated nutmeg or ground allspice
Pinch of ground cloves
1 9-inch prepared piecrust

Preheat the oven to 425°F.

In a large bowl, stir together all the ingredients except the piecrust. Pour the mixture into the pie shell.

Bake for 15 minutes. Reduce the heat to 350°F. and bake for about 45 minutes, or until the pie is set.

Preparing a Fresh Pumpkin

Wash a pumpkin and cut it in half through the middle. Remove the seeds and stringy center. Turn the pumpkin halves cut side down on a large baking sheet and bake at 325°F. for 1 hour, or until the flesh is tender. Scrape out the flesh and process it in batches in a blender or food processor fitted with the metal chopping blade until smooth.

Chapter 13

Happy Holidays!

········· ~ð~ ·········

I t comes as no surprise to us that some of our favorite recipes on "Live" have appeared on the shows during the holiday season. Whatever our faith may be, almost all of us have seasonal foods we like to serve at this most celebratory time of the year. And as we get together with our families and loved ones, the holidays come sweeping into our kitchens and homes, resulting in some wonderful recipes and ideas for entertaining and decorating.

For instance, character actor Vincent Schiavelli, who most of us would know from his roles in Ghost and Batman Returns, is a cookbook author and quite an accomplished cook. Vincent's grandfather, Papa Andrea, was a chef for a baron in Sicily before he moved to the United States. Once here, with Vincent at his side, he continued to cook for at least 18 family members every Sunday. His rich Fish Soup became a family Christmas Eve tradition that Vincent shared with the viewers of "Live."

Husband and wife cookbook authors Fred and Linda Griffith like to make loaves of wholesome Apricot-Cranberry Bread, which they give as presents during the holiday season. Restaurant consultant and cookbook author Rozanne Gold celebrates Hanukkah, the Festival of Lights, with an assortment of "little meals," featuring traditional potato pancakes in inspired new ways.

Almost certainly, you have holiday traditions of your own, and we hope that this chapter brings you recipes and tips that will inspire you to add some new ones.

Suppa 'i Pisci
(Sicilian Fish Soup)

V incent Schiavelli, character actor and author of *Papa Andrea's Sicilian Table,* shared his easy-to-make recipe for a delicious fish soup that has become a Schiavelli Christmas Eve tradition. After his family enjoys the soup, the second course is a traditional Sicilian assortment of fried fish and vegetables. Because this soup is much too good to experience only on Christmas Eve, Vincent recommends serving it at other times of the year with potato croquettes as an appetizer and an orange and fennel salad afterward. For dessert, he suggests rice pudding. (All these recipes are in his book.)

Vincent's sister-in-law, Joanne Rice, is a devoted viewer of "Live" and, prior to the show, she offered him a few pointers on how to tell if his recipe was a hit or not. If Regis takes more than one taste of the prepared dish, Joanne said, and doesn't invite Kathie Lee to taste the food, it's a winner. The day that Vincent was on the show, he was the last guest and they were running late. Vincent speedily and efficiently demonstrated the recipe in record time, Regis took his obligatory taste—and Vincent happily reports that Regis just kept on eating as the closing credits began to roll.

2 pounds fish composed of three different kinds, such as swordfish, shark, sea bass, cod, orange roughy

2 medium-sized onions, thinly sliced

2 cloves garlic, chopped

4 stalks celery, thinly sliced

4 sprigs Italian parsley, chopped

1 (28-ounce) can Italian plum tomatoes, drained of their liquid, coarsely chopped

1/2 cup extra-virgin olive oil

22 peppercorns

Sea salt
Black pepper
2 to 3 bay leaves
1 cup dry white wine

Cut the fish in pieces about 1 1/4 inches square. Leave them to soak in a bowl of cold salted water. This process will soften, sweeten, and remove excessively strong flavors from the fish.

Meanwhile, prepare the other ingredients. In an ovenproof casserole with a lid (earthenware is best), mix together all of the ingredients except the fish, bay leaves, and white wine. Be sure to add salt and pepper. Gently slip the bay leaves on the bottom of the pot so that they don't break. Arrange the fish on top, and moisten with the white wine. Add just enough water to barely cover the fish.

Cover and bake in a preheated 375°F. oven for exactly 40 minutes. Discard the bay leaves and serve.

Regis and actor Vincent Schiavelli discuss the finer points of cooking.

Swiss Lemon Pie

Makes 8 servings

T he refreshingly tart, tangy flavor of this lovely lemon pie would make it the perfect choice as a finale to a holiday meal. The top of the pie is decorated with lemon segments or slices brushed with an apricot-jam glaze. Experiment with cutting lemon slices into quarters or halves to form different designs. Regular guest Chef Tell is the creator of this recipe.

Piecrust to make a single 8- or 9-inch shell (you can also use
    a frozen store-bought pie shell)
4 large eggs
3/4 cup granulated sugar
2/3 cup freshly squeezed lemon juice
1/2 cup orange juice
Finely grated peel of 2 lemons (about 2 teaspoons)
1/4 cup unsalted (sweet) butter
1/4 cup heavy (whipping) cream
Lemon segments or thin slices of lemon for decorating the
    top of the pie
1/4 cup apricot jam
1 tablespoon water

P reheat the oven to 375°F. Bake the pie shell in a glass pie plate for 10 to 15 minutes, or just until it starts to feel firm, but has not started to brown. Transfer the pie plate with the partially baked shell to a wire rack.

M eanwhile, in a large bowl, stir together the eggs, sugar, lemon juice, orange juice, and lemon peel until combined.

I n a large saucepan, heat the butter and cream over medium heat until the butter is melted. Whisk in the egg mixture. Cook, stirring constantly, for 5 to 8 minutes, until the mixture is thickened. Cool slightly. Pour the mixture into the pie shell and bake for 20 to 25 minutes, or until the filling is thick and the crust is golden brown.

Transfer the pie to a wire rack and cool completely. Decorate the top of the pie with the lemon segments or lemon slices.

In a small saucepan, heat the apricot jam and water over medium-high heat. Bring the mixture to a boil and cook for 2 minutes, stirring occasionally, until it is slightly thickened. Cool the mixture slightly and brush it over the lemon segments or slices.

Home for the Holidays
~ 🦃 ~

- Select a theme for decorating your home so that everything sort of ties together. Some ideas: an old-fashioned country Christmas, Christmas at the beach, Victorian Christmas, wildlife Christmas. Children will enjoy helping to make ornaments and decorations to enhance the theme you choose.

- Entwine strings of fake pearls in evergreen wreaths.

- Circle each guest's plate with a ring of battery-powered miniature white lights.

- Apples provide a cheery Christmas motif. Fill silver bowls with polished fruits. Use inexpensive apple ornaments to adorn napkins. Use apple stickers on place cards. Look for apple-topped pencils, etc., as party favors for your guests.

- Substitute low-wattage pink bulbs for higher wattage white ones to make your guests look and feel warm.

- Make sturdy gingerbread people or Christmas trees. Before baking, cut a hole in the top of each cookie with a drinking straw. When the cookies are baked and decorated, thread a piece of ribbon through each hole and hang your cookie creations in the window. Or, of course, they too can be party favors.

Festive Roasted Green Apples
(aka Heavenly Regis)

Makes 4 servings

After chef Erik Blauberg prepared this recipe on "Live," Regis told him that the title, Festive Roasted Green Apples, just did not do this dessert justice, so Erik promptly renamed the dessert "Heavenly Regis." Certified Executive Chef Blauberg said that the dish was typical of the natural cuisine he served at the New York City restaurant, Colors.

Erik made this recipe in ring molds, which are available from restaurant supply stores, but he also suggested that you can use 10-ounce custard cups. He likes to serve the apples surrounded by blueberry or chocolate sauce along with a scoop of ice cream or sorbet and a garnish of fresh fruit.

While Erik was preparing the recipe, Regis took the stance of an investigative reporter and asked him if chefs do anything devious to meat that is sent back when it's not cooked to your liking. In his case, Erik reported he aims to please and only tries to make the customer happy.

5 Granny Smith apples
Juice of 1 lemon
2 tablespoons unsalted (sweet) butter, softened
2 tablespoons granulated sugar
1/4 cup almond flour (see Note)
1 large egg
1 tablespoon firmly packed brown sugar
Confectioners' sugar for dusting the tops of the desserts

Note: To make almond flour, combine equal amounts of almonds and flour and process in a food processor until smooth. Sift the mixture to remove any coarse particles.

Preheat the oven to 350°F. Place four 4-inch diameter by 3/4-inch deep ring molds or four 10-ounce custard cups on a baking sheet and spray with nonstick cooking spray.

Peel the apples and coarsely shred them. In a large bowl, toss the shredded apples with the lemon juice; drain off any excess juice.

In a small bowl, stir together the butter and granulated sugar until smooth. Stir in the almond flour until blended. Whisk in the egg until smooth. Stir this mixture into the shredded apples until combined. Press the mixture into the prepared ring molds or custard cups. Sprinkle the tops evenly with the brown sugar. Bake for 15 minutes or until lightly browned.

If you used the ring molds, carefully transfer the filled rings to dessert plates and remove the rings; set the custard cups directly on the plates. Lightly dust the tops of the desserts with confectioners' sugar.

Joanna, Jennifer, Joy, Cassidy, Regis, Kathie Lee, and Cody share a laugh in front of the Christmas tree.

Bugnes au Sucre
(Fried Cookies with Sugar)

Makes about 100 small cookies

Daniel Boulud, chef of Manhattan's Restaurant Daniel, prepared his grandmother's recipe for some delicate cookies. These diamond-shaped puffs would provide a delightful ending to any holiday meal. Restaurant Daniel is a favorite with Regis and Kathie Lee.

3 1/3 cups all-purpose flour
2 tablespoons granulated sugar
1 tablespoon finely grated lemon peel
Pinch of salt
3 large eggs, lightly beaten
6 tablespoons unsalted (sweet) butter, softened and cut into
    tablespoons
6 tablespoons sour cream, at room temperature
2 tablespoons vegetable oil
6 tablespoons water
Vegetable oil for frying cookies
Confectioners' sugar for dusting cookies

In the bowl of a heavy-duty electric mixer, stir together the flour, sugar, lemon peel, and salt. Make a well in the center of the flour mixture and pour the beaten eggs into it. Using the paddle attachment of the mixer, beat the flour mixture on low speed just until combined.

Distribute the butter pieces, sour cream, and 2 tablespoons of vegetable oil evenly over the top of the flour mixture. On low speed, beat until blended. Scrape the bottom of the bowl. Pour the water over the dough. On medium-low speed, beat the dough for 10 to 15 minutes, or until the dough is smooth and elastic. If necessary, scrape the dough off the paddle occasionally. (Turn off the mixer first!)

Gather the dough into a ball, lightly dust the surface with flour, and wrap tightly in plastic wrap. Refrigerate for 8 hours or overnight.

Pour enough oil into a large skillet so that it is 1 inch deep. Heat the oil to 350°F. While the oil is heating, roll out the cookies.

Cut the dough into quarters and keep the pieces refrigerated until ready to roll out. Pat a piece of dough into a square that is 1/16-inch thick. Cut the square into diamonds by cutting it into 1 1/2-inch-wide diagonal strips, first in one direction and then in the opposite direction.

Using a metal spatula, carefully lift the diamonds up and transfer them to a baking sheet lined with waxed paper. Refrigerate the diamonds until you are ready to fry them. (The dough is soft. Once chilled, you can gently stretch the diamonds back into shape if they get distorted while being lifted up.)

Fry the cookies about 12 at a time until they puff up and turn golden brown, about 2 to 3 minutes on each side. Transfer the cookies to paper towels to blot up excess oil. Cool slightly. Generously dust with confectioners' sugar. Repeat with the remaining pieces of dough, adding additional oil, if necessary.

Rita's Jelly Centers

This marvelously simple recipe for butter cookies is from segment producer Barbara Fight, and it has been in her family for four generations. Barbara remembers helping her grandmother make these cookies when she was a child and her grandmother would let her press her small thumb into each cookie's center to make the indentation. The cookies are named for Rita, Barbara's mother.

Barbara's tip for dinner parties is to keep hors d'oeuvres to a minimum. Everyone loves to eat them, she says, but by the time you are ready to sit down for dinner, everyone is full. She prefers to serve light hors d'oeuvres, such as raw vegetables and dips.

1 cup (2 sticks) lightly salted butter, at room temperature
1/2 cup granulated sugar
2 large egg yolks
2 1/4 cups sifted all-purpose flour
Jam or jelly for filling the centers of the cookies

Preheat the oven to 350°F.

In a large bowl, cream the butter until smooth. Gradually beat in the sugar. Beat in the egg yolks. Gradually beat in the flour.

Shape the dough into 1-inch balls. Place the balls about 2 inches apart on an ungreased baking sheet. Make a deep thumbprint in the center of each ball of dough. Fill each indentation with about 1/2 teaspoon of jam or jelly. Bake for 10 to 15 minutes, or until lightly browned. Transfer the cookies to wire racks to cool completely. Store the cookies in an airtight container at room temperature.

Holiday Memories
~❦~

*F*or the 1993 Christmas Eve show, Santa and Tannenbaum, an elf from the Radio City Music Hall Christmas Spectacular, paid a visit to the set of "Live" and recalled some of the gifts that Regis and Kathie Lee had received. Santa remembered that Kathie Lee had been delighted with a frilly tutu and that Regis had been the recipient of a spoon—a wooden spoon! (We're sure that it was meant for cooking purposes only.)

The Philbin and Gifford families (Frank was unable to be there) gathered to reminisce about past holidays. For her first appearance on "Live," Cassidy wore a plaid Christmas bow headband. Cody's gift to his new sister was a wreath. A holiday photo of the Gifford poodles, Chablis and Chardonnay, reminded Kathie Lee that the dogs had been a big part of their lives prior to the arrival of Cody and Cassidy.

The Philbins chuckled about making graham-cracker houses together, an activity later re-created as a cooking segment on the show. Joy also recalled that the year the family moved from California to New York, the girls really cleaned up on gifts at Christmas because she and Regis felt guilty about the move.

There were carols from a children's choir, and Regis and Kathie Lee sang a couple of holiday songs. Regis said, "You know, my family doesn't listen to me when I sing." Joy replied, "I guess we should, since people do pay to hear you!"

~❦~

Apricot-Cranberry Bread

Makes 2 loaves

Bright flecks of apricot and cranberry peek through the crust of this hearty bread created by the husband-and-wife authors of *The New American Farm Cookbook,* Fred and Linda Griffith. Well-wrapped, this bread will keep for a month or two in the freezer. A wrapped loaf atop a cutting board would make a thoughtful hostess gift. Linda and Fred report that you can cut the amount of butter by 1/2 cup for a lower-fat version; it will be a slightly drier yet still delicious bread.

1 1/2 cups unbleached all-purpose flour
1 cup whole-wheat pastry flour (available in health-food stores)
1 1/4 cups uncooked old-fashioned rolled oats
1 tablespoon baking powder
1 tablespoon ground cardamom
1 teaspoon ground allspice
1 1/2 cups unsalted (sweet) butter, softened
1 cup granulated sugar
1/2 cup firmly packed light brown sugar
3 jumbo eggs
2 cups chopped fresh cranberries
1 1/2 cups chopped dried apricots
Grated peel of 1 orange
1 1/2 cups milk
1/2 cup fresh orange juice
1/4 cup sour cream

Preheat the oven to 375°F. Thoroughly oil two 9 1/4-by-5 1/4-inch loaf pans.

In a large bowl, stir together the flours, oats, baking powder, cardamom, and allspice.

In another large bowl, using an electric mixer fitted with the paddle, beat together the butter and sugars until combined. One at a time, beat in the eggs, scraping the side of the bowl occasionally. Mix in the cranberries, apricots, and grated orange peel. Beat in the milk, juice, and sour cream until combined. Add the flour mixture and mix just until blended.

Divide the batter evenly between the pans, smoothing the surfaces. Bake for 50 to 60 minutes, or until a cake tester inserted into the center of each loaf comes out dry. Transfer the loaves in the pans to wire racks to cool for 5 minutes. Remove the loaves from the pans and cool completely. When the loaves are cold, store them in an airtight container at cool room temperature. This bread freezes well.

Holiday Entertaining Tips for Little or No Money from Rozanne Gold's Little Meals

~ℰ~

1. Tie long, thin breadsticks with ribbons.

2. Use beautiful lacquered chopsticks for all dishes with Asian flavors.

3. Create your own "condiment bar" on a tray that's passed around the table.

4. Instead of napkins, put large linen dish towels in napkin rings.

5. Use large plates, 10 to 12 inches, when serving one Little Meal; use 8-inch plates when serving a succession of Little Meals.

6. Use different plate patterns for every course.

7. Create your own wine tasting: Give every two guests their own bottle of wine. Encourage sharing.

8. Make place cards with funny sayings.

9. Have each guest bring a homemade dessert: This saves time and money and is fun for all.

10. Make something extra to give to your guests as they leave: cookies, candies, or spiced nuts wrapped beautifully.

11. Serve hors d'oeuvres and drinks in the kitchen.

12. If you have a very large kitchen, give everyone a task to do. You supply the aprons.

13. Make an edible centerpiece and draw numbers at the end of the meal to determine who gets to take it home.

14. Serve finger bowls with lemon slices.

15. Steam little white washcloths, rolled up, in your vegetable steamer, and pass them around after the meal.

16. Mix up a pitcher of "Arnold Palmers" for your friends who don't drink—half fresh lemonade, half iced tea.

17. Create a "coffee bar": Serve hot coffee accompanied by a tray with small bowls of shaved chocolate, whipped cream, cinnamon sticks, vanilla sugar, lump sugar, and several liqueurs.

18. Make two dramatically different desserts and serve them alternately to guests. This encourages sharing and conversation.

19. When you travel, collect wrapped sugar cubes from trips. Serve in a crystal bowl with hot drinks.

20. If your guests enjoyed a particular dish, have a calligrapher write out the recipe and send it to everyone who was there.

Little Meals for Hanukkah

Rozanne Gold, culinary director for the Joseph H. Baum & Michael Whiteman Company, a prestigious restaurant consulting firm, created a very special Hanukkah cooking segment for "Live" based on the concept of her book *Little Meals: A Great New Way to Eat and Cook.* She suggests selecting two or more recipes that reflect a theme or sentiment; "Use your table as a stage," she says, "and set it with imagination and flair." Her demonstration revolved around different presentations for the basic potato pancake recipe that follows.

Rozanne Gold's Potato Pancakes

Makes 4 to 6 servings

1 1/2 pounds potatoes, grated and squeezed dry
1 small onion, grated
1 egg, lightly beaten
2 to 3 tablespoons nonfat sour cream (or milk)
4 to 6 tablespoons all-purpose flour
1 teaspoon salt
Freshly ground black pepper to taste
Vegetable oil or a light olive oil for frying

In a large bowl, mix all the ingredients together to make a batter.

In a large skillet, heat about 1/2 inch of oil over medium-high heat until the oil is hot enough to brown the potato pancake mixture. Drop the pancake mixture by heaping tablespoonfuls into the oil. Cook the pancakes for 2 to 4 minutes on each side, or until golden brown on each side. Serve immediately, or place them in a warm oven until ready to use.

Silver Dollar Potato Pancakes
with Red Wine Applesauce

Makes 4 servings

5 large red apples (such as Red Delicious or Rome or a
combination)

1/3 cup granulated sugar

1/2 teaspoon ground cinnamon

3/4 cup sweet red wine or 1/2 cup sweet vermouth and 1/4
cup cassis

1 recipe of Rozanne Gold's Potato Pancakes

Fresh mint for garnish (optional)

Cranberry sauce or currant jelly for garnish (optional)

Peel and core the apples. Cut them into large wedges.

In a heavy medium-large pot, cook the apples, sugar, cinnamon,
and wine over medium-high heat. Bring the mixture to a boil, reduce
the heat to low, and cover. Cook 15 minutes, uncover, and cook for 5
to 10 minutes longer, or until most of the liquid has evaporated. Mash
the mixture lightly with a potato masher, leaving some chunks of apple.
Chill well.

Follow the pancake recipe, making 16 to 20 small pancakes.
Place them in a warm oven. When ready to serve, mound red wine
applesauce in the center of the plate. Surround the sauce with 4 to 5
little pancakes. Garnish with fresh mint and a small amount of cranberry sauce or currant jelly.

"Napoleon" of Smoked Salmon and Potato Pancakes

Makes 4 servings

1 recipe of Rozanne Gold's Potato Pancakes
8 large slices of smoked salmon
2 Kirby cucumbers, thinly sliced
1/4 cup finely chopped fresh dill
1/4 cup crème fraîche or nonfat sour cream

Follow the pancake recipe, making 8 medium-large pancakes. Place them in a warm oven.

Place 1 warm pancake in the center of each of 4 large plates. Top each pancake with 1 slice of smoked salmon, another potato pancake and another slice of smoked salmon. Arrange the sliced cucumbers around the "Napoleon." Sprinkle with chopped dill and top each with 1 tablespoon of crème fraîche or nonfat sour cream

Christmas at the Giffords

Kathie Lee: We live in a 1760s farmhouse in Connecticut—it looks just like a Currier and Ives postcard—and every Christmas we have our dearest friends over for a buffet supper with old-fashioned caroling. We have over one hundred people now, so we set up two buffets—one downstairs in our game room and one up in our dining room. We serve old-fashioned turkey, stuffing, and mashed potatoes. Our friends have told us that the party means a lot to them. I think that as Christmas becomes more and more commercialized, people long for ways to celebrate in the true spirit of the season.

My Vegetable-Potato Pancakes

1 recipe of Rozanne Gold's Potato Pancakes
1 large carrot, coarsely grated
1 medium unpeeled zucchini, coarsely grated
3 tablespoons grated Parmesan cheese
1/2 cup ricotta cheese
1/4 cup finely chopped red bell pepper
Fresh basil leaves, for garnish

In a large bowl, prepare the ingredients for the pancake recipe. Stir in the carrot, zucchini, and Parmesan cheese. Form the mixture into 4 large vegetable-potato pancakes.

In a large skillet, heat about 1/2 inch of vegetable oil over medium-high heat until hot enough to brown the pancakes. Cook the pancakes in the hot oil for about 5 minutes on each side, or until crisp and browned.

Put 1 pancake in the center of each of 4 large plates. Top each pancake with 2 tablespoons of ricotta cheese. Sprinkle the top of each pancake with the red pepper and garnish with the basil.

Holiday Tips from Martha Stewart
~❧~

When it comes to holiday gift-giving, it's hard to beat Martha Stewart's stylish homemade gifts. Martha made an appearance on "Live" during December and showed some of her great ideas. Here are a few that you might want to include in your own holiday celebrations.

Stamp tissue paper with a festive rubber stamp and use it to line gift baskets that contain one or all of the following items. Buy clear cellophane in big rolls. Surround the baskets with big pieces of cellophane, tied together at the top with a beautiful ribbon.

Homemade Scented Sugars. Layer fragrant vanilla beans and granulated sugar in decorative jars. The sugar will absorb the flavor of the beans and create a delightful sugar that is wonderful for use in coffee, tea, and baked goods. You can also use this principle to create sugar flavored with strips of lemon peel (let the peel dry out for a day before adding it to the sugar). These sugars can be used as you would regular sugar. Tie the glass jars with handsome bows.

Potpourri. Purchase small corsage bags at your florist and pack them with your own blend of homemade potpourri. To boost the aroma of the potpourri, sprinkle with essences of aromatic oils, which can be purchased at local health food stores and often nurseries.

Beeswax Candles. You can easily make your own beeswax candles in the size(s) of your choice. Purchase wicks and sheets of beeswax at a craft store. Select a length of wick and trim the sheets of beeswax accordingly. Tightly roll the beeswax around the wick, gently squeezing the layers together as you roll to form a nice shape.

Paper Whites. These narcissus flowers are very satisfying to grow, because you can almost see them sprout up right in front of your eyes! Simply assemble a wide, shallow clay dish with enough small pebbles to fill it. Place the paperwhite bulbs, root end down, in the pebbles. Fill the dish with enough water to cover the pebbles—not completely submerging the bulb. You can use moss as a decorative covering, placed around the bulbs over the pebbles. Keep the level of water consistent at all times.

Sweet Apple-Potato Pancakes
with Apple Chips and Honey

3 large red apples
1 recipe of Rozanne Gold's Potato Pancakes
3/4 cup granulated sugar, divided
1/2 teaspoon ground ginger
1 teaspoon grated orange peel (optional)
About 1 pint of vanilla ice cream
6 tablespoons honey
Confectioners' sugar and ground cinnamon, for garnish
   (optional)

Preheat the oven to 200°F. Very lightly grease a baking sheet. Cut 2 of the apples into paper-thin slices, removing any seeds.

Place the apple slices on the prepared baking sheet and bake for about 2 hours, turning once or twice. The apples will dry out and curl up a little bit.

In a large bowl, prepare the ingredients for the pancake recipe. Peel, core, and coarsely grate the remaining apple. Stir in the grated apple, 1/2 cup of the sugar, the ginger, and the orange peel, if desired, until combined. Form the mixture into 12 pancakes.

In a large skillet, heat about 1/2 inch of vegetable oil over medium-high heat until hot enough to brown the pancakes. Cook the pancakes in the hot oil for 3 to 4 minutes on each side, or until crisp and browned. Sprinkle each pancake with 1 teaspoon of the granulated sugar and place them in a warm oven. (If desired, you can brown them under the broiler for 30 seconds.)

To serve, place 2 apple-potato pancakes on each plate. Serve with 2 to 3 of the prepared apple chips and a small scoop of ice cream. Drizzle each serving with 1 tablespoon of honey. Sprinkle with confectioners' sugar and cinnamon, if desired.

The "Live with Regis & Kathie Lee" backstage family poses for a group photo. From left to right: (back) Cindy MacDonald, segment producer; John Verhoff, free-lance segment producer; Delores Spruell-Jackson, segment producer; (on sofa) Rosemary Kalikow, segment producer; Cynthia Lockhart, production secretary; Michael Gelman, executive producer; Isabel Rivera, audience coordinator; Joanne Saltzmann, segment producer; (front) David Mullen, production assistant. Not pictured: Barbara Fight, segment producer; Suzy Hayman-DeYoung, assistant producer; Kathleen Gold-Singer, on-air promotion manager; Robin Shallow, production executive.

$\mathcal{R}$esources

To get tickets to "Live with Regis & Kathie Lee," send a postcard with name, address, and phone number to:

"Live" Tickets
Ansonia Station
P.O. Box 777
New York, NY 10023-0777

To write to Regis and Kathie Lee:

Regis Philbin and/or Kathie Lee Gifford
"Live with Regis & Kathie Lee"
7 Lincoln Square
5th Floor
New York, NY 10023

To get "Live"'s newsletter, send $2.00 plus a self-addressed, stamped envelope for each issue:

"Live" Newsletter
Issue #——
P.O. Box 2010
Floral Park, NY 11002

To enter "Live"'s Trivia Contest, mail a postcard with your name, address, and phone number to:

"Live" Trivia Contest
Ansonia Station
P.O. Box 108
New York, NY 10023

For The Clever Cleaver Brothers' cookbook and videotapes, write to:

Clever Cleaver Productions
968 Emerald Street, Suite 51
San Diego, CA 92109
or call (800) 658-5830

Cookbooks

Francis Anthony. *Cooking with Love: The Love Chef Shows You How.* Henry Holt & Co. 1990.

———. *Cooking with Love, Italian Style.* Hearst Books Division of William Morrow. 1994.

Lidia Bastianich and Jay Jacobs. *La Cucina di Lidia.* Doubleday. 1990.

Daniel Boulud. *Cooking with Daniel Boulud.* Random House. 1993.

Stephen J. Cassarino and Lee N. Gerovitz. *Cookin' with The Cleavers.* Wynwood Press. 1990.

Dean Fearing. *Dean Fearing Southwestern Cuisine: Blending Asia and the Americas.* Grove Weidenfeld. 1990.

———. *The Mansion on Turtle Creek Cookbook.* Grove Weidenfeld. 1987.

Bobby Flay. *Bobby Flay's Bold American Food.* Warner. 1994.

Pierre Franey. *A Chef's Tale.* Alfred A. Knopf. 1994.

——— and Bryan Miller. *Cuisine Rapide.* Random House. 1989.

Rozanne Gold. *Little Meals: A Great New Way to Eat and Cook.* Villard Books. 1993.

Fred and Linda Griffith. *The New American Farm Cookbook.* Viking Studio Books. 1993.

Lauren Groveman. *Lauren Groveman's Kitchen: Nurturing Meals for Family and Friends.* Chronicle Books. 1994.

Kermit the Frog, as told to Robert P. Rieger. *One Frog Can Make a Difference: Kermit's Guide to Life in the 90's.* Pocket Books. 1993.

Robin Leach. *The Lifestyles of the Rich and Famous Cookbook: Recipes and Entertaining Secrets from the Most Extraordinary People in the World.* Viking Studio Books. 1992.

Pino Luongo. *A Tuscan in the Kitchen: Recipes and Tales from My Home.* Clarkson Potter. 1988.

Joan Nathan. *Jewish Cooking in America.* Alfred A. Knopf, Inc. 1994.

———. *The Jewish Holiday Kitchen.* Schocken Books. 1989.

Joseph E. Orsini. *Father Orsini's Italian Kitchen.* St. Martin's Press. 1991.

Paul Prudhomme. *Chef Paul Prudhomme's Seasoned America.* William Morrow & Company, Inc. 1992.

———. *Fork in the Road.* William Morrow & Company, Inc. 1993.

Vincent Schiavelli. *Papa Andrea's Sicilian Table: Recipes from a Sicilian Chef as Remembered by His Grandson Vincent Schiavelli*. Birch Lane Press. 1993.

Dinah Shore. *The Dinah Shore American Kitchen*. Doubleday. 1990.

Martha Stewart. *Pies and Tarts*. Clarkson N. Potter, Inc. 1985.

Jeremiah Tower. *Jeremiah Tower's New American Cuisine*. Harper & Row. 1986.

Todd Wilbur. *Top Secret Recipes: Creating Kitchen Clones of America's Favorite Foods*. Penguin USA. 1993.

Janos Wilder. *Janos: Recipes and Tales from a Southwest Restaurant*. Ten Speed Press. 1989.

Sylvia Woods and Christopher Styler. *Sylvia's Soul Food*. William Morrow & Company, Inc. 1992.

Prize Winners from the
"Live"/Good Housekeeping's
Favorite Family Recipe Contest

~ℰ~

 In the summer of 1994, right before this book went to press, "Live" and *Good Housekeeping* magazine sponsored a recipe contest. Of all the submissions, the following five recipes were the finalists with Heidi's Original Carrot Cake sent in by Heidi L. Harrison being the grand prize winner. Each finalist appeared on "Live" and demonstrated their favorite family recipe. The judging panel of Michael Gelman (Executive Producer of "Live"), Mildred Ying (*Good Housekeeping*'s Food Editor), The Love Chef, Francis Anthony (frequent "Live" guest chef), and Michael Lomonaco (head chef of New York's "21" restaurant) made the final selection on Friday, July 15th, 1994. The grand prize winner won a year's worth of groceries. We wanted to include these recipes in this permanent collection because they are perfect for entertaining.

Heidi's Original Carrot Cake

Makes 10 to 12 servings

2 1/4 cups all-purpose flour
2 heaping teaspoons ground cinnamon
2 teaspoons baking soda
1 teaspoon salt
1/4 teaspoon nutmeg
1/4 teaspoon ground allspice
2 cups sugar
1 1/4 cups vegetable oil or canola oil
3 large eggs
2 teaspoons vanilla extract
2 cups shredded carrots (about 3 large carrots)
2 cups flaked coconut
1 cup chopped pecans
1 cup raisins
1 (8-ounce) can crushed pineapple in juice
Additional pecan halves, for garnish (optional)

Preheat the oven to 350°F. Generously grease and flour three 8-inch round cake pans.

In large bowl, with mixer at medium speed, beat sugar, oil, eggs, and vanilla until mixed. Add flour, cinnamon, baking soda, salt, nutmeg and allspice; beat until blended. With spoon, stir in the carrots, coconut, pecans, raisins and pineapple. Pour the mixture into the prepared pans and bake 30 to 35 minutes until a knife inserted in center comes out clean. Spread some Cream Cheese Frosting (recipe follows) between cake layers and frost top and side of cake with remaining frosting. Garnish with pecans, if desired.

CREAM CHEESE FROSTING

12 ounces cream cheese, softened
1/4 cup milk
1 teaspoon vanilla extract
3 to 4 cups confectioners' sugar

In large bowl with a mixer at medium speed, beat together the cream cheese, milk, and vanilla until smooth. Gradually beat in just enough of the confectioners' sugar to make the mixture spreadable.

Heidi L. Harrison
Oceanside, California

Greek Spinach Pie

- 1/4 cup olive oil
- 1 onion, chopped
- 1/2 bunch dill, chopped (optional)
- 4 10-ounce packages frozen chopped spinach, thawed and squeezed dry
- 4 large eggs
- 2 cups crumbled feta cheese
- 1 8-ounce package cream cheese, softened
- 1 16-ounce package fresh or frozen (thawed) phyllo
- 1/2 cup unsalted butter (1 stick), melted

Preheat the oven to 350°F. In a 10-inch skillet, heat the olive oil. Add the onion and dill and cook for 5 to 7 minutes, or until the onion is softened. In a large bowl, combine the cooked onion mixture, thawed spinach, eggs, and the cheeses.

In a 13-by-9-by-2-inch glass baking dish, layer 10 sheets of phyllo dough, lightly brushing each sheet with some of the melted butter. Spread the spinach/cheese mixture evenly over the surface. Top with 15 more sheets—once again brushing each sheet with the melted butter. With a sharp knife, cut into servings each about 2 inches square. Bake for about 50 minutes, or until golden brown. Serve warm, cooled, or cold—it will have your family raving for more.

Anna S. Paraskeva
Miami, Florida

Breakfast Pizza

Makes 8 to 12 servings

2 packages refrigerated Pillsbury crescent dinner rolls
10 large eggs, beaten
1/2 cup milk
1/2 teaspoon dry mustard
1/2 teaspoon black pepper
1 pound ground sausage (pork or turkey) cooked until
  browned and drained of fat
or
1 pound cooked ham, cubed or shredded into pieces
2 to 3 cups Hash Brown O'Briens (these include onion and
  pepper)
2 to 3 cups shredded cheddar cheese
Grated Parmesan cheese (optional)

Preheat the oven to 375°F. Lightly grease a 15 1/2-by-10 1/2-inch jelly roll pan (with sides). Unfold the crescent dinner rolls into strips and place them on the bottom of the pan. Using your fingers, pat the strips together and up the sides of the pan. In a large bowl, whisk together the eggs, milk, mustard, and pepper. Sprinkle the sausage and potatoes evenly over the crescent rolls. Sprinkle the cheese evenly over the top. Carefully pour the egg mixture over everything.

Let the egg mixture settle into other ingredients. If desired, sprinkle Parmesan cheese over the surface. Bake for 40–45 minutes until the pizza is solid with no liquid in the center. (The time will vary with the oven.) Let the pizza cool slightly and cut into squares. Serve with a fresh fruit salad and you're ready for the raves.

Bari Landorf
Naperville, Illinois

Michael's Summer Pasta

1 to 2 tablespoons vegetable oil

2 (4-inch long) hot Italian sausages (can substitute mild), cut into 1/2-inch pieces

6 medium-large ripe tomatoes, cored and diced

6 large garlic cloves, peeled and finely chopped

1 medium-sized onion, finely diced

1 large cucumber, peeled, seeded and cut into 1/2-inch cubes

1 large (15 ounces) green zucchini, peeled and diced

8 ounces mushrooms, stems removed and caps sliced*

4 ounces fontina cheese, cut into bite-sized cubes

4 ounces Bel Paese cheese, cut into bite-sized cubes

1 tablespoon dried basil leaves

2 teaspoons dried oregano leaves

2 tablespoons extra-virgin olive oil

1/4 teaspoon hot pepper sauce (optional)

1 pound penne pasta

1 tablespoon high-quality Parmesan cheese, grated

In a large skillet, heat the oil over medium-high heat. Add the sausage and cook for 7 to 10 minutes or until completely cooked through. Using a slotted spoon, transfer the sausage to paper toweling and drain well. In a large bowl, combine all the other ingredients except the pasta and Parmesan. Let stand at room temperature for at least an hour or in the refrigerator overnight. Cook the pasta in boiling water until al dente according to package directions. Drain the pasta (Do not run cold water over it.)

Pour the combined ingredients over the hot pasta. Toss well to combine. Sprinkle the Parmesan cheese over the top and serve.

Serve with a nice tossed salad with any good Italian dressing, and with a nice bold Chianti wine. Any leftovers can be chilled and served cold as a refreshing pasta salad.

Michael Avre
Oakland, California

*Reserve stems for use in soup stocks, etc.

Hawaiian Fruit Salad
with Banana Dressing

Makes 8 servings

1 pineapple
1 medium cantaloupe
1 medium honeydew melon
1 papaya
1 mango
1 kiwifruit
1 cup strawberries
1 cup seedless green grapes
Leaf lettuce

Remove the top from the pineapple. Cut the pineapple lengthwise into fourths. Trim the peel and "eyes" from the pineapple. Remove the core. Cut the pineapple into 2-by-1-inch pieces. Using a melon baller, cut balls from the cantaloupe and honeydew. Cut off peel and slice papaya, mango, and kiwifruit. Cut each strawberry lengthwise in half. Arrange all the fruits on the leaf lettuce. Serve with Banana Dressing (recipe follows).

BANANA DRESSING
2 ripe bananas, peeled and sliced
1 cup sour cream
1/4 cup firmly packed brown sugar
1 1/2 teaspoons lemon juice

Add all the ingredients to the container of a blender or food processor. Cover and process for 12 to 15 seconds until smooth. Refrigerate for up to 2 hours.

Kacy Furey
Oakland, California
(originally from Waipauh, Hawaii)

Index